Here's all the great literature in this grade level of *Celebrate Reading!*

Flights of Fancy
Journeys of the Imagination

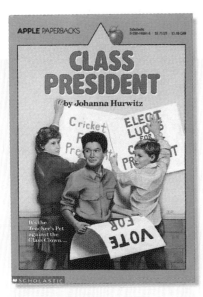

Featured Poet
Natalia Belting

Before Your Very Eyes

A World of Nature

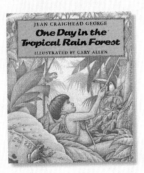
Featured Poets
Marilyn Singer
Byrd Baylor
George David Weiss
Bob Thiele

Many People, Many Voices

Stories of America

Featured Poets
Duke Redbird
Linh To Sinh My Bui

Within My Reach

The Important Things in Life

Handle with Care

Making a Difference

Featured Poets
Ouida Sebestyen
Danny Williams

BOOK F

Ask Me Again Tomorrow
Growing and Changing

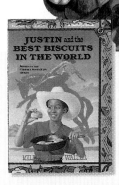

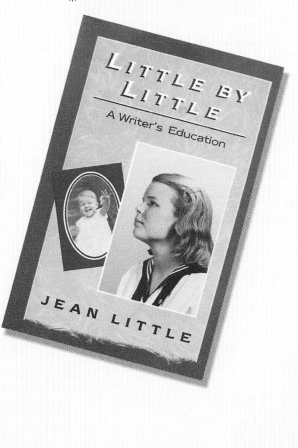

Celebrate Reading!
Trade Book Library

The Great Gerbil Roundup
by Stephen Manes

**Wayside School
Is Falling Down**
by Louis Sachar
☀ Children's Choice
☀ Parents' Choice
☀ Garden State Children's
Book Award

The Year of the Panda
by Miriam Schlein
☀ Outstanding Science Trade
Book for Children

Shiloh
by Phyllis Reynolds Naylor
☀ Newbery Medal

Taking Care of Yoki
by Barbara Campbell

A Lion to Guard Us
by Clyde Robert Bulla
☀ Notable Social Studies Trade Book

The Trading Game
by Alfred Slote
☀ Notable Social Studies Trade Book
☀ Library of Congress
Children's Book

A Taste of Blackberries
by Doris Buchanan Smith
☀ ALA Notable Children's Book
☀ Georgia Children's Book Award

The Pinballs
by Betsy Byars
☀ ALA Notable Children's Book
☀ Children's Book Award
☀ Notable Social Studies
Trade Book
☀ California Young Reader Medal
☀ Library of Congress
Children's Book

Number the Stars
by Lois Lowry
☀ Newbery Medal

The Secret Garden
by Frances Hodgson Burnett
☀ Lewis Carroll Shelf Award

The Noonday Friends
by Mary Stolz
☀ Newbery Medal Honor Book
☀ ALA Notable Children's Book
☀ Library of Congress
Children's Book

Within My Reach
The Important Things in Life

About the Cover Artist
Elizabeth Wolf lives in Washington, D.C. with her
husband and two children. She enjoys illustrating
theater posters and children's books.

ISBN 0-673-81160-3

1997
Scott, Foresman and Company, Glenview, Illinois
All Rights Reserved.
Printed in the United States of America.

Acknowledgments appear on page 136.

1 2 3 4 5 6 7 8 9 10 DQ 01 00 99 98 97 96

Within My Reach

The Important Things in Life

ScottForesman

A Division of HarperCollinsPublishers

Contents

GOLDEN OPPORTUNITIES

LOST AND FOUND
Genre Study

STUDENT RESOURCES

The Night over

Sky Kansas

from **THIN AIR**
by *David Getz*

The Night Sky over Kansas cost $1.98. Though it would leave him with only two cents, Jacob felt it was worth it. He could use it for a practical joke on his older brother, Isaac. And it was the whole sky. It was the moon, Mercury, Venus, Mars, Jupiter, and Saturn. It was all the constellations. It was three hundred stars, the Milky Way, and Halley's Comet. It was all some farm boy in Kansas could see if he stood out in the middle of his wheat field on a clear August night and looked up.

Jacob would attach the pieces of the Sky onto the ceiling above Isaac's bunk. Each stick-on planet, star, and galaxy was guaranteed to glow in the dark. Isaac wouldn't notice anything while his light was on. But when he turned it off, his ceiling would fly backwards toward infinity, and the entire universe would open up above him.

Isaac would be frightened, but it might give him and Jacob something to talk about for a change.

Standing on his toes in front of a display of cookbooks for cat owners, Jacob lifted the Night Sky into the air so that the clerk behind the counter could see it. The clerk, whose bald head was shaped like a light bulb, leaned over the counter and brought his face within an inch of Jacob's. The clerk's eyes bulged. He had a long, wispy mustache. He smelled like the basement of Jacob's building. Jacob's nose itched. He scratched it with the corner of the Sky. He put his two dollars down on the counter.

D·9

"It's our last Sky," the clerk said.

"I won't drop it," Jacob promised.

Out on the crowded, noisy street, surrounded by all of Manhattan, Jacob clutched the package to his chest. He was surprised by how light the Sky felt in his hands. He was delighted. He had something to look forward to again.

He had gone to sleep the night before looking forward to his first day of sixth grade in his new school and showing his parents he could succeed in a regular class. But he got an asthma attack in the middle of the night. He sprang upright in his bed, trying to wake, gasping for air. He was wheezing and coughing. Not for the first time, he thought he was dying. Slowly he began to wake. He took his asthma spray. He started his breathing exercises. He needed to relax.

Isaac helped by panicking. He scrambled down from his top bunk and sat at the edge of Jacob's bed, looking bug-eyed and pale. He was wearing his blue Rangers jersey, number eleven.

"How come you don't sleep with the helmet on too?" Jacob asked, pulling his knees up to his chest. He breathed out slowly. He coughed. He told himself that if he relaxed, if he stopped wheezing, he could make it to school in the morning.

Isaac called for their mother. He started to dial all of the emergency numbers at once.

"When was the last time you took your theophylline?" Isaac asked. His voice was deep for a fourteen-year-old's. He sounded almost like their father, except their father never panicked.

"Call 555-1313," Jacob gasped.

Isaac quickly dialed the number.

It was Sportsphone.

"How did the Mets do?" Jacob asked, still wheezing.

IT'S OUR LAST SKY.

"Ma!" Isaac called. He hung up the phone. "Jacob, what's Dr. Grophy's number at St. Vincent's Hospital?"

Their mother rushed into the room.

"Ma, he's wheezing," Isaac said, going over to the closet to get his clothes.

Jacob took another inhalation from his spray.

"Jacob, are you all right?" his mother asked.

Holding his breath, keeping the medicine inside him, Jacob nodded yes. He was almost enjoying himself. Watching Isaac in a frenzy distracted him from his own problem: breathing. Isaac's performance, his mother rushing in, first to help him, then to calm Isaac, made him think of his routine asthma attack as an exciting, amusing movie. It even made him laugh, until he began to worry about its star.

"Isaac, where are you going?" his mother asked.

Isaac had put his baseball jacket on over his jersey. Jacob was surprised at how tall his brother was, nearly a head taller than their mother.

"Are we going to the hospital?" Isaac asked.

"Why don't *you* go like that," Jacob suggested. Isaac was still wearing his jockey shorts. "I'll meet you there later." He put his head on the pillow. He was going back to sleep. He did not want to be tired for his first day of school.

When Jacob's alarm sounded at seven, he was already dressed. Though tired and weak, he was still eager to get to school. He was going to be in a regular class, not that Special 10 class his parents wanted him to be in. They had completed the enrollment papers just before moving from their Lower East Side neighborhood to the Upper West Side.

"I'm not going into any special program," Jacob had told his parents. "There's nothing special about me."

"Jacob, it's a great program," his mother had argued. "It's designed especially for kids like you who miss too much school."

"It's only for bright kids," his father said.

"Bright kids like you, who have chronic illnesses."

I DON'T HAVE A CHRONIC ILLNESS.

"I don't have a chronic illness," Jacob argued. "I'm the same as everybody else. I just have asthma."

"Jacob, you missed over forty days of school last year," his mother said.

"I'll miss more if you put me in that class," Jacob threatened. "I won't go. I'm not ill."

His parents backed down. His father agreed to bring him over to P.S. 89 to register him in a regular class in the sixth grade. But it would be an experiment. If his health held up, if it didn't look as if he was going to miss too many days of school, he could stay.

Getting dressed, to Jacob, meant getting ready to prove himself. In his new school nobody would know he had asthma. Nobody would treat him as if he were disabled. He would be a new kid. He began to lace up his new black high-tops.

"Jacob, where are you going?" his mother asked, entering his room.

"School?" he guessed.

"I don't think that's a very good idea."

"Why not?" he asked. "Lots of kids do it. It keeps them out of trouble."

"I don't think you should exert yourself," she said, sitting down beside him. "It might trigger another attack."

"But . . ."

It was too late. She began The Speech.

"Jacob, you have sensitive lungs," she said, "and you probably have a germ. If you go to school, your germ is going to get a chance to meet all of those other germs hiding out in those other kids in your class. Those kids could be walking germ factories. I'm sure their mothers don't even think twice of sending their kids to school with a germ."

"Ma, what do you think they do?" Jacob asked. "Pack it with their lunches?"

"Pneumonia, strep throat, the flu, doesn't worry these mothers."

"But, Ma . . ."

"Look, Jacob. If you do have a germ—and I don't think we can take a chance, not with you—your germ is definitely going to be the type that invites all those other germs living happily in those other kids to come over to your lungs to have a party."

"But, Ma . . ."

"And suddenly there's going to be a party in your chest, and you're going to get your bronchitis, and instead of a day, you're going to miss the first two weeks of school."

"But . . ."

"You have to stay away from potential infections."

"But those potential infections are my potential friends!"

She ordered him to stay in bed, to rise only to take a glass of apple juice or some chicken soup from the pot. "This way, you'll only miss one day," she said, pouring the apple juice into six eight-ounce glasses, which she placed in the refrigerator. She removed a frozen chunk of "emergency" soup and placed it in a sauce pan on the stove.

"I'm going to school tomorrow," Jacob insisted.

"I'll stay home with him today, Ma," Isaac offered.

Jacob looked up. He had almost forgotten his brother. Then he realized Isaac had been there all along, quietly waiting for his opportunity to be the wonderful older brother.

"No, you won't," Jacob said.

"It's only the first day of school, Jacob," his mother said. "Maybe it's not such a bad idea."

"It's a bad idea," Jacob said,

...THREE HUNDRED STARS, THE MILKY WAY, AND HALLEY'S COMET.

glaring up at Isaac, whose broad shoulders and eager face reminded Jacob of some sheriff's son in a western. He was wearing their father's old tattered junior-varsity hockey jacket. "It's a very bad idea."

"No, I'll enjoy it," Isaac said, removing his jacket and putting down his books. "We'll have a good time."

"But not too good of a time," his mother cautioned.

"Put your jacket back on, Isaac," Jacob ordered. "Go to school. You have your after-school hockey tryouts today."

"No, it's okay," Isaac said, hanging up his jacket. "They last all week."

"Don't hang up that jacket, Isaac."

"I don't understand you," his mother said, sitting down beside him. She rubbed his back. "Why is it such a

I DON'T UNDERSTAND YOU.

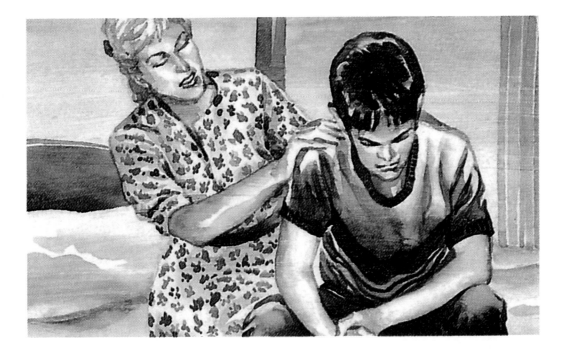

bad idea if your brother stays home and takes care of you?"

"Because . . . because . . . because he'll be good to me! He'll talk to me! He'll read to me. He'll tell me jokes. He'll turn on the television. He'll switch the channels for me. He'll heat up the soup and hold the spoon for me!" He pointed a finger at Isaac, as if accusing him of some horrible crime. "He'll take care of me!"

Isaac responded to the accusation with a proud smile. "You want me to take down Blue Line Hockey from the closet?" he asked.

"See!" Jacob cried out in frustration. "He enjoys it! It makes him happy. He enjoys taking care of me!"

"Now, why is that bad?" his mother asked, looking confused.

"Because, Ma, when he takes care of me, he . . . he makes me feel like a sick person."

"But you are," his mother sighed. "You probably have a germ."

"Ma, if he stays home, I'm going to school. And I'm walking up to every kid I see with a runny nose, watery eyes, and a cough, and I'm going to ask them to breathe on me."

"Jacob, sometimes I really don't think you have a very good idea of what's best for you," his mother said.

"I don't need somebody to hold my spoon."

Isaac took his jacket out of the closet and picked up his books. "You sure you don't want me to stay home and play Blue Line?" he asked.

WHY IS IT SUCH A BAD IDEA IF YOUR BROTHER STAYS HOME AND TAKES CARE OF YOU?

"Go to school, Isaac," Jacob said.

"Look, Jacob, I'm putting your medicines here," his mother said, sitting down on the bed beside him. She removed two pills from their childproof vials and placed them on top of the *Mad* magazines on his desk. "I wrote down when you're supposed to take them."

Jacob turned away and stared at the wall. "I'll take the two pills right after breakfast," he announced. "If I start wheezing, I can take the spray."

"Take the two pills right after breakfast," his mother said. "And if you start wheezing, take the spray."

"And your number and Dr. Grophy's number are on the refrigerator. I'll call if I need anything. Now go to work. You're going to be late." He sat up.

"Don't exert yourself, Jacob. I don't want you bringing on another attack. Stay in bed." She kissed him, then turned the television to face his bed. She pulled out the knob to turn the set on, but turned off the volume.

"Why did you do that?" he asked.

"This way, if you want to watch television, all you have to do is turn the volume switch."

"Ma, please go to work. Isaac, go to school. I can take care of myself."

"I'll phone you between classes," Isaac said, holding the door for their mother.

"I'll phone you this morning. And don't get out of bed if you don't have to," his mother said as they left. She locked the door from the outside.

As soon as he heard their footsteps going down the stairs, Jacob got out of bed. He was going to school.

It was the first day of school. He couldn't miss it. He couldn't let the year start without him. He'd be late, but at least he'd get there. He'd have to wait a few minutes, though, before he made his escape. His mother could come rushing back to the apartment in five or ten minutes, just to remind him to drink his juice or to use a teaspoon and not a tablespoon for his cough medicine. He turned the television off and took out his favorite sick-day book, *Legends of Crime*. He propped up his pillows, leaned back, and opened to the chapter on Billy the Kid. He began to read about Billy's mother when he remembered he had to eat breakfast if he was going to take his medicine. If he took his pills on an empty stomach, they would make him queasy and nervous. He noticed there was a plate of fruit on the end table. His mother must have put it there when he wasn't looking. He picked up an apple. It fell apart in his hand. His mother had sliced it into tiny, bite-sized sections. He lost his appetite. He also noticed he was wheezing again.

He returned to his book. He read how Billy had been scrawny but dangerous. His wheezing was getting worse. He put the book down and took his spray. His breathing cleared for a minute or two, but then he started to wheeze again. He took another dose of his spray. It didn't work.

If he relaxed, if he did some breathing exercises, maybe he could open his lungs. Then he could go to school. He didn't want to miss lunch. He didn't want to miss being on somebody's team during recess. He sat up

...BECAUSE HE'LL BE GOOD TO ME!
HE'LL TAKE CARE OF ME!
HE'LL READ TO ME.
HE'LL TELL ME JOKES...!

straight, his
back to the wall.
Hugging his knees
to his chest, he tried
to blow out all of the air
in his lungs. He coughed and gasped.
He was getting that dry, scratchy feeling inside. Again he
hugged his knees to his chest and tried to blow all the air
out of his lungs. He couldn't. It was getting difficult to
breathe. He didn't want to have another attack.

He didn't want to have to call his mother or brother.
He didn't want to feel helpless. He took his pills. He would
have to wait to see if they worked.

He thought about his father. He was in Chicago, playing the part of Zachary in *A Chorus Line*. He was expected home in two weeks for a short stay. His father said he didn't enjoy being away from his family, but it was the money he earned acting in regional theaters and touring companies that had allowed them to move out of their drug-infested old neighborhood.

"What can I do?" his father would apologize to Jacob every time he packed his bags. "All I can do is act."

It was his father's traveling that paid for Jacob's medicine, his doctor and hospital bills. Jacob understood that, but didn't accept it. His father was his only friend. They went to the movies and museums together, worried about the Rangers and Mets, laughed at the same jokes, and never mentioned his asthma. Sometimes his father

HE'LL HEAT UP THE SOUP
AND HOLD THE SPOON FOR ME!
HE'LL TAKE CARE OF ME!

even forgot what foods Jacob was allergic to, or when he
was supposed to take his medicines. But that was all right.
Jacob remembered.

In two weeks his father would be home. Jacob
wondered what he could do to convince him to stay?

His heart was racing. His lungs were clear, but his
heart was racing.

It was the pills, he reassured himself. His hands were
trembling. It was just the pills, he told himself. Yet he was
beginning to feel nervous. He tried to read, but he couldn't
hold the book still. He was frightened.

He turned on the television for company. People
dressed up like chickens and monkeys were jumping up
and down, begging for money. He changed the station. "I
just spoke to the doctor," a woman whispered. "There are
signs of foul play." He changed the channel. Mister Rogers.

Mister Rogers was speaking to the camera. Very slowly. "Well . . . isn't that colorful? What do we see? Pie . . . pie . . . and blueberries for pie."

He turned off the set. He put his high-tops back on. He took his baseball jacket from the closet. Realizing he had to put something into his stomach, he grabbed a handful of pretzels from an open bag in the refrigerator and stuffed them into his jacket pocket. He took his keys and left, slamming the door behind him. He ran down the five flights of steps.

Outside, his back against the building, he lifted his face to the sun. It warmed him, calmed him. He listened to the street sounds for companionship. The bickering of cars and trucks, the wailing of an ambulance siren, the sound of salsa music coming from a window above, all helped make him feel less alone.

He began to walk towards school, munching his pretzels. He stopped. His mother and brother were going to call in an hour or so. If he didn't answer the phone, they would both send ambulances and then come flying home.

He decided to get the *Times* before going back upstairs. Maybe the new play his mother was in had been reviewed. He could check to see if the Mets had won.

The Mets had lost. The play wasn't reviewed. Back at his building, he stuck his hands into his jacket pocket and pulled out a handful of pretzel crumbs. His keys were gone. He was locked out. Within an hour his mother and brother would call home. He had to get back into that apartment.

He ran back to the newsstand where he had purchased the *Times*.

"I'm sorry," Jacob said, trying to get the man's attention.

"What are you sorry about? You don't like the news in that paper I sold you?"

"No. I lost my keys."

"So you want a newspaper that tells you where to find them?"

"No. Do you mind if I look through your newspapers to see if they fell out when I paid you?"

"Go ahead and good luck."

"Thanks." Jacob began to sort through the magazines and newspapers. He looked on the ground beneath and on the sides of the booth. No keys.

"You sure you didn't see me drop them?"

"Even if you did drop them, I wouldn't have seen it. I'm blind."

"Oh, I'm sorry," Jacob said, backing away.

"Don't be sorry. Why aren't you in school?"

"I had an asthma attack."

"Oh, I'm sorry," the dealer said.

"You don't have to be sorry. I'm all right."

"Me too," said the dealer.

Jacob started walking back home. He couldn't call his mother. Her phone number was on the refrigerator. He wasn't even sure if she was at work or downtown at some theater, rehearsing. And he couldn't call his brother. It would be just another great excuse for Isaac to come to the rescue.

He thought of running away from home. He couldn't. His asthma medicine was back up in the apartment. He couldn't survive the night without it.

He shuddered as he pictured the ambulances, police cars, his mother and brother, all flying towards his building. Imagining the anxious and confused look on his mother's face when she saw him, perfectly happy, sitting on the front steps of his building, made him feel flushed and ashamed.

He would have to call Isaac. The phone booth was in front of the bookstore. He figured he had at least fifteen minutes. They sold used books inside. Maybe he could find something funny, something to make him laugh.

Instead, he found the Night Sky over Kansas.

He also found his keys. They were on the ground, by the phone booth. They must have fallen out of his pocket when he pulled out his change for the newspaper. He ran home.

The phone was ringing as he entered the apartment. He picked it up.

"How's your germ?" It was his mother.

"He's not here right now. Who's calling, please?" he said as he darted to the refrigerator, grabbed the three apple-juice glasses his mother had left him, and poured them into the sink.

"Jacob, don't be sarcastic with me. How are you feeling?"

"Fine. A little tired. I had to turn the volume knob way up and it took a lot out of me."

"Jacob, don't make me come home and punch you in the nose. Are you feeling better? Say yes."

"Yes."

"I don't believe you. How many glasses of apple juice did you drink?"

"I finished off three."

"Good. Go back to sleep. I love you."

"I love you too, Ma."

He hung up the phone. The phone rang. He picked it up.

"I'm fine, Isaac," he said, and hung up.

Grabbing the Night Sky, he climbed up to Isaac's bunk. For the next three hours he crouched on his brother's mattress, map of the Night Sky on his knees, wetting the backs of tiny planets, moons, and hundreds of stars and sticking them in their places on the ceiling. Laughing to himself, he imagined Isaac's expression as he turned off his reading light and the Night Sky over Kansas exploded above.

That evening Isaac got into bed and, as usual, read for about an hour. Jacob knew Isaac was reading a novel about a boy who had overcome some horrible physical ailment to become an Olympic athlete. He knew because Isaac occasionally read aloud to him, though Jacob asked him not to. All Isaac ever read were books about athletes who had had to overcome horrible disabilities.

"Hey, Jacob, let me read you this."

"I'm tired, Isaac, and your light is keeping me awake."

I'M TIRED, ISAAC, AND YOUR LIGHT IS KEEPING ME AWAKE.

"I'll turn it off. All you had to do was ask. You feeling well enough to go to school tomorrow?"

"I felt good enough to go today."

"Jacob, wake me if you have any problems breathing."

"Good night, Isaac."

"Good night, little brother. Sleep well."

The lights clicked off.

Silence. Jacob stared up into the thick, cloudy darkness that floated beneath Isaac's bunk. He waited. He wondered. Was Isaac mute with terror, or was he asleep?

Jacob gently scratched at the low ceiling made by the wooden slats supporting Isaac's bunk. No response. He got out of bed and climbed the ladder up to the top bunk.

Isaac was asleep. Jacob sat down at the foot of the bed, careful not to wake him. He drew his knees up to his chest and surveyed the Sky, which glowed quietly, almost distantly, above him. He listened to the strong, clear sound of Isaac's breathing.

Imagining himself as that boy in Kansas, out by himself at night in that vast wheat field, Jacob looked up and suddenly felt very much alone.

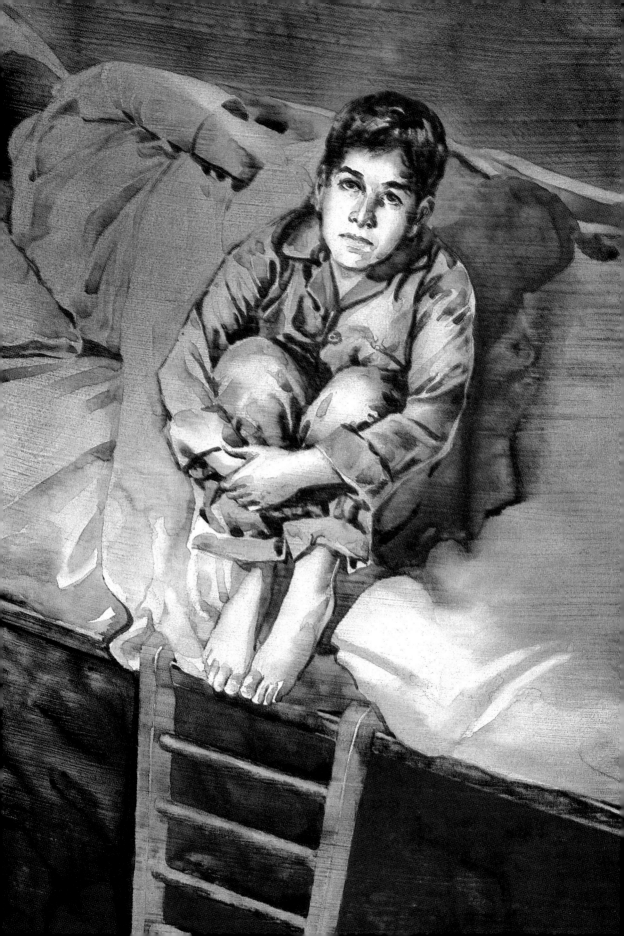

THINKING ABOUT IT

1

Jacob wants to be independent. Does this sound familiar?
Have you ever tried to convince someone to allow you to
be more independent? Did things work out for you as they
did for Jacob? Explain your answer.

2

Even though he cares for his mother and brother, Jacob
feels his father is his only friend. Why is that?

3

Imagine that Jacob becomes friends with the man at the
newsstand and visits him whenever he can. What do you
think they talk about?

Alone In The Nets

from *Sports Pages* by Arnold Adoff

I
am
alone   of   course,
    in the nets, on this cold and raining afternoon,
    and our best defending fullback
    is lying on the wet ground out of position.
    Half the opposition is pounding
                                down the field,
                and their lead forward is gliding
                so fast, she can just barely keep
                the ball in front of her   sliding
                                                foot.
Her cleats are expensive,
and her hair $b_ou_nc_es$
                    neatly
like the after
        girls   in the shampoo commercials.
                    There is a big grin
                            on her face.

D · 33

Watch Me On The Wing

from *Sports Pages* by Arnold Adoff

Sweeper: the deeper I can play
        the faster I can lay
out my traps for their fullback
moving too close to mid   field.
I shine along the side   lines
           from mid   field
           back to our goal.

I am the quickest,
        sharpest,
most intelligent,
(and
most m o d e s t ,) player on
               my
               team:
        in this league.

I have the
superspeed.
I have the need to do a little
more
than play only one position. I
defend. I score. I run like
wind
across the corn fields of
this
town.
I am a brown tornado on a
muddy
day.

The opposition knows
I come to play   with
all I bring. They
watch:

w a t c h   m e   o n   t h e   w i n g .

Skybird to the High Heavens

A story of Guatemala
by Nancy White Carlstrom

MY NAME IS ROSA. ROSA LUCAS PAIZ. I ONCE LIVED IN A LAND WHERE FOOTBRIDGES DANGLED HIGH ABOVE RUSHING STREAMS AND MOUNTAINS STRETCHED UP GREEN TO THE SKY. SOMEHOW THE COWS KEPT FROM FALLING OFF THE STEEP CLIFFS.

My name is Rosa. Rosa Lucas Paiz. I once lived in a land where footbridges dangled high above rushing streams and mountains stretched up green to the sky. Somehow the cows kept from falling off the steep cliffs.

"Grandmother, who keeps the cows in place?" I asked when I was a young girl.

"The same one who keeps the sun in the sky," my grandmother answered as she sat weaving on the floor of our house.

Corn grew in my land. Corn grew in patches on the side of the mountains where the cows did not fall. Grandmother said corn was one of the most important things we had. Corn gave us life.

My grandmother taught me how to weave. She had pieces of old weavings her grandmother gave to her when she was a girl. One day, she took them out and showed me.

"Rosa, these are the designs of our people." And she explained to me how each village used certain colors and designs in the weaving of cloth.

"I have saved these samples for many years, so I could pass them on to you. When I die, you will have them to use as patterns, so our own special weaving will live on."

As Grandmother taught me to weave, she told me stories about our land and its living things.

"Grandmother, tell me again about the time you saw the quetzal."

And Grandmother told me yet another time about when she was a girl and traveled far to the lowlands with her family. There, as they passed through the jungle, Grandmother had glimpsed the most beautiful bird in the world. The quetzal had blue-green tail feathers that stretched out three feet long. On its head was a tuft of gold and its chest wore a blood-red vest.

"If only I could see a quetzal someday, Grandmother."

"Maybe you will, my child. Maybe you will."

That night, I dreamed I rode on the back of a quetzal. I felt the rush of the wind as we soared to the high heavens. In the morning, I told my grandmother about my dream.

"How could I ride a quetzal, Grandmother?" I asked. "Did the bird become large, or did I become small?"

"Perhaps the dream was telling you that soon you must become small and hide from the danger wandering through our land. No matter what happens, may you always remember the sweet smell of the earth, my child."

I knew my grandmother was talking about the war that was tearing our country apart, like a hideous beast. But still, I did not fully understand her warning.

And so, all morning as I did my chores, I daydreamed about becoming small. Small enough to hide behind the clay cooking pots my mother kept by the fire. Maybe if I jumped out I could surprise her and make her laugh.

I could be small enough to hide in an ear of corn and watch the sun glow on my father's back as he lifted the hoe.

...grandmother told me yet another time about when she was a girl and traveled far to the lowlands with her family. there, as they passed through the jungle, grandmother had glimpsed the most beautiful bird in the world. the quetzal had blue-green tail feathers that stretched out three feet long. on its head was a tuft of gold and its chest wore a blood-red vest

"Father, why do you spend so many hours weeding the corn?" I asked, when he came home with rough hands and a tired back.

"Why, Rosa, if I allow the weeds to grow, the souls of the corn plants will move to cleaner fields. Then what would we eat, my daughter? How could we trade to buy the tools we need, the sandals you wear on your feet?"

"Sell the stories Grandmother tells as she weaves on her loom," I said with a laugh.

Father just shook his head, but Grandmother smiled to herself and I knew she would tell me another tale later, when the crickets sang.

That night, Grandmother told me of the great earthquake that leveled our village before I was born. She told me how the houses folded like paper and how giant rocks were tossed from the mountains like pebbles. It was a sad, true story.

"We thought the sun would fall from the sky that time. But it didn't, Rosa," she said quietly.

"Grandmother, when you saw the quetzal in the jungle, did you want to catch him and bring him home?"

"No, Rosa, I knew the quetzal was a bird of freedom. A cage would kill him. There are other ways to enjoy his beauty."

That night, my dreams were troubled. I could not ride the quetzal to the high heavens. I could not hide behind my mother's cooking pots or in the corn of my father's field.

"Where will I go?" I cried. "Where will I go?"

In the morning, soldiers came and burned our village. First, I hid. Then, as the whole sky turned black, I ran and ran. I could not look back.

My name is Rosa. Rosa Lucas Paiz. I now live in a place far from where the footbridges dangle above the rushing streams and the mountains stretch green into the sky.

"Grandmother," I whisper, "the cows have fallen off the cliff. The sun has dropped from the heavens and the corn rots."

I miss the corn that gave me life. I miss the pot of water my mother kept boiling all day on the fire. I miss the hoe of my father chopping in time with our people for hundreds of years. I miss the stories my grandmother told and the threads of color she wove on the loom.

"Grandmother," I whisper, "what if I forget the sweet smell of the earth? What if they put all the quetzals into cages?"

This morning, as I walk to the place where I work in the refugee camp, I am surprised to hear someone call my name.

"Rosa." The voice is thin, like burnt paper, almost ready to crumble into little pieces.

"Rosa."

It comes to me across the miles that I have traveled while running in the cold night and burning day—fleeing through the cornfields, meeting up with others from distant villages, living pressed up close, finding shelter together from the winter rains. I see again a shared blanket, a cup of water and warm tortillas passed around, and these are like sparks of light in the darkness of my memories.

"Rosa, Rosa, is that you, dear?"

And there before me is a shriveled little woman dressed in the *traje* of my village: María Magdalena Rivas, my grandmother's friend. Tears stream down my face.

Here is someone who knew my mother who kept the fire going, my father who lifted the hoe, my grandmother who told the tales and wove the cloth.

And now I sob at my loss, and in the arms of that old, familiar woman from my village, I take comfort.

She reaches deep under the belt that wraps around and around her frail body and takes out a small packet, a packet worn from the journey she has made.

Inside are the sample pieces of weaving, the designs of our people. The pieces handed down by my great-great-grandmother. The ones my grandmother wanted me to have.

As I hold them in my hand, I see the brilliant colors, blue-green, gold, and red—colors of the beautiful bird from the land I love. I know then that I will not forget. I will weave our patterns, designs of light, no matter where I live. I want the world to know and remember too.

"Grandmother," I whisper, "maybe it will keep the cows on the cliffs and the sun from falling. And just maybe tonight I will ride the quetzal, my skybird to the high heavens."

Thinking About It

1

Rosa cherishes her grandmother's weavings and the memories they represent. Describe something you cherish from when you were very young. What memories come to mind?

2

Sometimes an author will use an object to represent an emotion or belief. For example, the eagle is often used to represent freedom. What does the quetzal bird represent in this story?

3

Rosa has asked you to help preserve her memories of life with her grandmother. What can you suggest?

Another Book About Memories

Childhood memories really do come alive in *The Wonderful World of Toys* by Anna Braune.

A Fair Trade

by Sid Fleischman

From Mr. Mysterious & Company

ILLUSTRATED BY Eric Von Schmidt
LETTERING BY Laurie Rosenwald

*a*s his name suggests, Mr. Mysterious is no
ordinary man. His family is no ordinary family either:
Mr. Mysterious (Pa) and Mama and their children
Jane, Anne, and Paul travel around the Old West in a
covered wagon putting on magic shows in towns called
Cactus City and Dry Creek. In fact, the Mysterious
family is remarkable in every way save one—the
children want a dog and are bound and determined to
get one, no matter what Pa or Mama or anyone else
says about it.

Pa heard a dog bark.

"It must be a squeak in the wheels," he said. "We've got two horses, a cow and six rabbits, but we don't have a dog."

"Yes we do!" Jane laughed, snapping her fingers at the dog farther back in the wagon. "And he can do tricks. Sit up!"

Pa turned and saw a black dog sitting up on Mama's trunk.

"Can we keep him, Pa?" Anne begged.

Pa stopped the wagon in front of the livery barn and the dog climbed into Jane's calico lap. Pa shook his head. "That's a fine-looking dog, but he belongs to someone here in Lone City. We can't take him with us." Pa climbed to the ground. "Hand him to me, sister."

Sadly, Jane handed down the dog. His tail started wagging, stirring up a breeze, and he began to lick Pa's face—red beard and all.

"Now don't you go trying to break our hearts," Pa said. "You can't come along. You belong here in Lone City. Now get along home."

Pa mounted the wagon seat once more, and the dog sat in the hot dust. His tail was still.

"Git up, Hocus. Git up, Pocus."

Pa was silent a long time. The young 'uns had always wanted a dog, he knew, but it would only be another mouth to feed. There was no place in the show for a dog. All the animals earned their keep; Hocus and Pocus pulled the wagon, Madam Sweetpea gave fresh milk, and the rabbits popped out of hats. A dog was just a dog.

Jane tried not to look back. No one said a word, and there wasn't a smile on even one of the five faces. The wagon creaked and swayed along the rutted trail, and finally a sign appeared:

It was Mama who broke the silence, when she glanced behind to make sure Madam Sweetpea was still tied to the wagon.

"Look—he's following us," she exclaimed.

They all turned to look. The dog was indeed following in Madam Sweetpea's tracks.

Pa stopped the wagon and strode to the dog.

"Now see here, little dog. You don't belong to us. You go along home."

The black tail wagged a half circle in the dust.

"Hear me, little dog? You turn around and get home."

The tail stopped wagging. Pa took the reins once more, and the wagon lurched forward. But every time someone glanced behind, the black dog was

Jump! Jump, doggy!

there, following in Madam Sweetpea's tracks.

"He likes us," Jane said. "He wants to come along."

"Maybe he's trying to run away from home," Paul said.

"Andrew," Mama said. "His tongue is hanging out. All that walking in the sun and dust—he's thirsty again."

Pa leaned back on the reins once more. He sat a moment thinking hard, and the children held their breath. Then he tapped his hat firmly in place. "All right," he said. "There's no point in sending him home when we're so close to Cactus City now. Get him in the wagon. We'll find his owner and return him."

"Jump!" Anne shouted. "Jump, doggy!"

"Here!" Paul added.

"In the wagon!" Jane called out.

The dog leaped into their laps. Everyone was smiling again. The wagon moved on, and the children scraped another dipper of water out of the barrel.

The sun sat on the horizon like a huge pumpkin. The rooftops and false fronts of Cactus City stood on a mesa covered with cactus.

Much as the children had traveled, they had never seen so much cactus in one place in their lives. It was like driving the wagon through an enormous pincushion. Jane saw barrel cactus as big as nail kegs. Paul cast an eye over beavertail cactus by the dozens. Anne watched jumping cactus, hoping to see one jump. They didn't jump fast enough so that you couldn't get out of the way; in fact, Pa said they didn't really jump at all, but grew in leaps and bounds. Mama saw pancake cactus, which hardly looked good enough to eat, even with butter and molasses.

The whole town was waiting for the wagon show when Hocus and Pocus, lifting their white legs smartly, led the spinning gold wheels along the main street.

"There they are!" went up the shout. "Here comes Mr. Mysterious and Company!"

Pa lifted his stovepipe hat and the youngsters waved to the crowds along the boardwalks. The show wagon traveled the length of the main street. Folks in the hotel leaned out of the upstairs windows to watch. Boys and girls followed along the street (some of them doing cartwheels out of pure joy). They were dressed in their best calicos and homespuns. The ladies wore bustles and some of them carried parasols.

Pa halted the wagon across the very end of the main street and the townspeople gathered around. The show had been promised for seven o'clock sharp, which was just ten minutes away. There wouldn't be time to go to the general store—there wouldn't even be time for supper.

A man wearing a heavy silver watch chain across his ample vest stepped forward and raised his arm. The townsfolk quieted to a whisper.

"As mayor," he said, "I welcome you folks to Cactus City. Where's the show going to be?"

"In this very spot," Pa said. "With your permission, Mayor."

The mayor nodded. "Our young 'uns have been waiting all afternoon. We figured you got lost."

"We drove into Lone City by mistake."

"Don't stand there, jawin', Mayor!" someone shouted. "Let's get on with the show."

Pa pulled out his gold pocket watch. "My timepiece here says seven minutes to seven. We've been on the trail all day and we're a mite dusty. But our handbills promised you a magic show at seven o'clock sharp—and by gosh and by golly we'll give it to you!"

With only seven minutes to set up their props, the family had to work fast. Everyone had a job to do. Mama flew to the wooden trunk for their show costumes. Jane unpacked the colored silk scarves and flags her father would produce from "empty" vases and tin tubes. Paul set up the magician's table with the red velvet drape and the gold fringe. Anne brushed the lint off her father's black tail coat.

Pa rolled up a side piece of the canvas cover and let down a wooden side section of the wagon itself. It folded out like a tabletop to rest on two stout legs, and formed the stage. Then he lit the four kerosene footlights to be set out when the show started.

Inside the wagon a backdrop was hoisted and screens set up like stage wings. Jane changed into her pink gingham, and Paul buttoned up his blue assistant's uniform. Pa shifted Mama's portable piano behind one of the wings, and she took her place on the stool.

"All ready?" he whispered to his show company.

There was a nod all around, and Pa slipped into his tail coat. Everyone forgot about the black dog. In the rush and confusion he darted between Pa's legs and across the stage.

"Hey! That's my dog!"

A man shouldered his way forward. Anne peeked out and saw him first. Her heart began to race at the sight of him. He wore wide suspenders and a dirty hat, and his face whiskers stuck out like the quills of a porcupine.

"You there!" he shouted. "Come out here! You stole my dog Blue!"

Blue had disappeared behind the wagon drapes and was hidden, shaking and whining softly, behind a trick box.

Then the man climbed right up on the stage. Jane peeked out from one side and Paul from the other. The kerosene lamps lit up the man's face, and it was something fierce to see. The next thing Paul knew, the man had caught hold of his arm with a grip like a vise and yanked him out from behind the wings.

"You there!" the man growled. "You're nothing but a pack of rawhiders and thieves—even you young 'uns. Trying to make off with my dog!"

"Honest, mister—" Paul protested.

Pa strode out in his tail coat and stovepipe hat—and he looked even more angry than the stranger. "Take your hand off that boy," he said in a voice so sharp it could have split a rock.

The man turned, and his whiskers shook. "Where's my dog? Trying to hide him, were you?"

"Not a bit. He followed us with his tongue hanging out. He wouldn't turn around and go home. We figured his master would be here in Cactus City, so we let him come along. Sister, bring him out."

"Oh, you're not fooling Jeb Grimes," the man snapped. "I'm onto you actor folks. I'll get the sheriff and have you all thrown in jail!"

"Where's my dog?"

Jane picked up Blue and hugged him tight. There was a quick tear in her eye. She was sorry that he had to go home with the whiskered stranger. But she did what she was told. She set Blue at his master's feet. Almost at once the dog backed and growled.

"Come here, you lazy critter," Jeb Grimes said.

But Blue kept growling and then hid under Jane's long skirt.

Jeb Grimes faced Pa again. "You put a hex on my dog," he growled. "You turned him against me."

"No," said Pa. "Maybe you turned him against yourself. But he's yours and there's not much I can do. Now take that fine dog and get off this stage."

But Jeb Grimes planted his stout legs firmly where he stood and peered out at the townspeople. "Sheriff Johnson—you're out there, and you seen it for yourself. These show folks tried to steal my dog!"

The sheriff moved through the crowd. The star pinned to his vest glinted like silver. He leaned his big hands on the edge of the makeshift stage. "Jeb, you've got your dog back," he said. "Now stop making a fuss. These people look to me like they're telling the truth. That dog of yours follows everyone but you."

"They had Blue in their possession, sheriff—and that's thieving."

"Maybe and maybe not," Pa said. Jane had never seen his eyes so narrow and hard. "Take off your hat, Mr. Grimes."

"What?"

"Remove your hat, sir."

"What in tarnation for?"

"You just said possession is thieving."

"Well, it is."

"Then do me the kindness to take off your headgear."

Jeb Grimes squinted and looked around him, and the sheriff said, "What are you afraid of, Jeb? You hiding all your gold pieces under your hat?"

"I'm a poor man," Jeb Grimes declared, and everyone laughed—the folks from Cactus City as well as Lone City. They all knew he hoarded every dollar that came his way.

Finally he took off his old and battered hat. Pa beat the dust out of it and then rolled up his right sleeve. Very slowly he reached his hand deep into Jeb Grimes's hat—and pulled out a live and kicking white rabbit!

The townspeople gaped in amazement. They were so startled they forgot to applaud.

But Pa didn't perform the trick for applause. He was still simmering with anger. "Now then, Jeb Grimes," he said, "what are you doing with my rabbit hidden in your hat? Sheriff—that's thieving!"

Now the audience burst into a roar of laughter and whistling. Everyone laughed but Jeb Grimes.

He grabbed back his hat and pulled it down almost to his ears. "Blue!" he shouted. "Come here, you ornery, ungrateful critter."

"Just a moment," Pa said. "Mr. Grimes, I'd like to buy your dog."

"He ain't for sale," Jeb Grimes said.

At that moment the watch in Pa's vest pocket struck the hour. It was show time.

Pa lifted out the watch, and the chimes sounded again and again—seven times. The chimes were clear and beautiful—as golden as the watch itself.

Jeb Grimes's eyes opened in wonder. He had never seen a chiming watch before. Pa had bought it in Kansas City.

"Blue ain't for sale," he said again. "But that's a mighty pretty gold watch you got there. Rings out like a church bell, don't it?"

"Get off the stage, Jeb Grimes!" someone yelled. "Let's have the show."

But Jeb Grimes didn't move. "Yes sir, a mighty fine watch." He scratched through his beard. "I'd like to have a watch like that, mister. You want my dog? I might trade for that watch of yours."

Pa closed his hand over the watch. He had saved a long time to buy it, and he needed a timepiece. There wasn't another watch like it within five hundred miles, and he didn't want to give it up. But then he glanced at Jane and Paul and Anne peeking out from the wings. And he could even see Blue sticking his muzzle out from under the hem of Mama's dress, where he was now hiding.

All their eyes were on him. A dog didn't belong in the show, and he ought to leave well enough alone.

"It's a trade!" Pa said firmly. He unclasped the watch from his chain and put it into Jeb Grimes's gnarled hand.

"Not just the watch," Jeb Grimes said. "The chain too. Or it ain't a bargain."

"Jeb Grimes," Pa declared. "You must have been raised on sour milk. Here, take the chain and get off this stage."

Not just the watch....

"The chain too."

With that, he strung the chain loose from his fancy vest, which Mama had decorated with fine needlework. He dropped it into Jeb Grimes's waiting hand. Sorry as the children were to see Pa lose his watch and chain, it meant Blue would never again have to go home to Jeb Grimes.

"Blue!" Jane said. Her face lit up with sheer happiness. "Blue! You're ours!"

And Paul grinned, "You can come out now."

Blue crept out from under Mama's skirts and began to wag his tail once more. And Pa raised both arms to the audience.

"Folks!" he announced, and he was smiling again, "The show is about to begin! We present for your amusement, edification and jollification our traveling temple of mysteries! A program of wonders and marvels for young and old! Feats of legerdemain and tricks of prestidigitation! Magic, mirth and music!"

At this, Mama struck up a heavy chord on the small piano, and Paul, his buttons gleaming, hurried out with Pa's black wand.

"Folks!" Pa continued, with a gesture of the wand. "I present—MR. MYSTERIOUS AND COMPANY!"

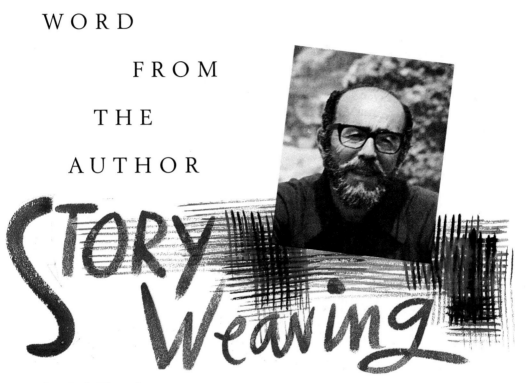

Story Weaving

by Sid Fleischman

One summer afternoon, when my children were young, I decided to make them a playful gift. I'd write a book just for them.

I'd make them the characters in the story, and put in our dog (whose real name was Buster Blue), and take them on an adventure.

But what adventure? I had no idea what the story would be. Since I'd once been a professional magician, it occurred to me to write about the world of magic that I knew so well. And as I had just finished a great deal of research on the Old West, I'd place the story on the frontier.

I sat down at the typewriter that afternoon and snapped the reins on Mr. Mysterious's red and gold show wagon, starting it on its travels. When I finished the first chapter, I called together the real Jane, the real Paul, and the real Anne and read the pages aloud. They were enchanted to be in a book!

But then I explained that I hadn't yet figured out the story. Did they have any suggestions for things that could happen? Yes, they did! And that became the pattern for the writing of the novel. As I finished each chapter, their ideas came popping out. Some I was able to weave into the story.

What began one summer's afternoon as a gift to my youngsters became a greater gift from them to me.

I had always written for adults. After *Mr. Mysterious & Company* was published, I found myself with an audience of children. Their letters, reacting to the story, began dropping into my mailbox. And it delights me that some of these readers have grown up to become magicians!

What began one summer's afternoon as a gift to my youngsters became a greater gift from them to me. For they led me into the joyful world of children's books. It's here that I have the most fun, a bit like Mr. Mysterious himself, conjuring up stories.

Thinking About It

 In "A Fair Trade," Mr. Mysterious doesn't think the family can afford an animal that doesn't earn its own keep. Have you ever wanted something that others might call useless? What happened?

 Jeb Grimes accuses the family of theft by saying, "possession is thieving." How does Mr. Mysterious turn this statement around to accuse Jeb?

 Saving Blue is a close call for the Mysterious family. The approach is clever, but it might not work again. Describe another way they could have saved Blue.

Another Book by Sid Fleischman Take another adventure courtesy of Mr. Fleischman: read *The Whipping Boy*.

Land of Promise

from
The Great American Gold Rush
by Rhoda Blumberg

The year is 1850. Gold in the new territory of California
is said to be so plentiful, you can scoop it out of the
riverbanks with a spoon and fork. California is called the
Land of Promise, and thousands decide to take her up on
that promise: there's gold to be had, and everyone wants a
share. The great American Gold Rush is on!

Swarms of overland travelers headed for Sutter's property, where gold had first been found. Marshall, the carpenter who discovered gold, had tacked notices along the American River claiming the land for himself, but people ignored his signs.

> ## "Swarms of overland travelers headed for Sutter's property, where gold had first been found."

Newcomers didn't even respect Sutter's property. They trampled his fields, dug up his grounds, and camped on his land. Sutter was horrified as he witnessed this free-for-all invasion. Sutter's twenty-two-year-old son, August, who hadn't seen his father since he was eight years old, emigrated from Switzerland in 1848 to work for him. He was shocked at the situation. "Everything belonging to my father was at everybody's disposal," he remarked.[1] August tried to salvage whatever he could by selling lots in New Helvetia. Buyers became the founders of present-day Sacramento.

San Francisco was the chief port for argonauts who came by sea. Because there were no docks, ships dropped anchor offshore in the wide harbor. Hundreds of ships were so close to one another that it took a skilled captain to steer without crashing into another vessel.

Small boats usually surrounded newly arrived ships. Some, acting as ferries, were quickly filled with customers willing to pay any price to reach shore. Others wcre occupied by businessmen eager to exchange bags of gold for imported products they could sell for profit. There were also San Franciscans who rowed out hoping to find servants. In one case, competing bids for a ship's cook ran as high as three hundred dollars a month, a tremendous salary at that time.

Heading for California

The harbor was jammed with ships abandoned by entire crews who had left for the diggings. Seeing so many deserted vessels was a shock. Passengers received more shock waves after landing. The beach was littered with mirrors, statues, stoves, kegs of coffee, cases of tobacco, cartons of clothing, and crates of cumbersome mining machines. Newcomers soon realized that they, too, had to dump

belongings: no porters to serve them; no carriages to move their supplies; no wagons to load their furniture; no servants to care for their clothes.

There were hotels in town where customers slept on wooden planks and tabletops. The hills were covered with tents and shanties because camping out was cheaper and less crowded.

San Francisco and harbor in 1851

MEALS

EAGLE SALOON

STO

D · 70

Abandoned ships were made into hotels and stores.

D-71

San Francisco grew with incredible speed. Prefabricated houses shipped from China, Europe, and the East Coast were assembled in one day. In 1848, there were approximately eight hundred people in San Francisco. In 1849, there were at least fifteen thousand, and by 1850, twenty-five thousand.[2] San Francisco became an important commercial center. New York and New England merchants profited enormously by sending shiploads of goods needed by gold-hunters who owned little more than a pick and shovel. They advertised

San Francisco during the winter of 1849.

their merchandise in newspapers throughout California's gold area.[3]

San Francisco was a stopover, a supply center, and a place to relax. Gambling houses and drinking saloons were everywhere. Streets were strewn with garbage. There were no sanitation or sewage systems. Nevertheless, San Francisco dirt seemed promising to a few people, who idled away their time picking gold flakes in the street—small pickings that probably fell out of miners' bags or were swept from shopkeepers' floors.

All the glitter was bright and encouraging until people noted prices. Inflation was sky-high. Shopkeepers collected gold faster than miners could dig it. Onions and potatoes sold for one dollar each. Eggs were ten dollars a dozen. Tacks were exchanged for their exact weight in gold.

> "*Eggs were ten dollars a dozen.*"

A shot of whiskey cost a pinch of gold, and milk cost even more than liquor. Laundry service was so expensive that bundles of dirty clothes were reportedly shipped to China or Hawaii, where they were washed and returned at "$8 a dozen."[4]

Miners returning from the diggings brought in bags, bottles, and buckets of gold. Stories got around about single panfuls of dirt worth two thousand dollars. Treasure was said to be underfoot on land and underwater in streams and rivers. However, many heard that the richest diggings had already been claimed. "There is gold here, but most of the fortunes are obtained, and what is left will require hard and constant labor," one forty-niner wrote.[5] Prospectors headed for the Sierra hills, hoping that depressing reports were deliberately created by successful miners who wanted to discourage competition.

Companies broke up as men decided to try their luck on their own. They didn't want to share the wealth they expected to find. And they wouldn't have to obey leaders, abide by laws, and stay with the same crowd. California was not only a land of riches, but also a place of freedom. No officials to stop them, no family to shame them—an ideal place to live without rules.

Diggings were scattered along the western slopes of the Sierra Nevada.[6] *Lode deposits* were in quartz veins deep in the ground. *Placer deposits* consisted of gold dust, flakes, and nuggets scattered through sand and gravel. During the early days of the Gold Rush, placer gold was the only kind known. Picks and shovels were the usual tools for uncovering buried treasure. No need for complex techniques. Just dig until the dirt shows yellow.

This merchant claims his food is worth its weight in gold.

Panning in rivers and streams was the simple, popular method. It sounded so easy: Swish a little gravel and water around in a container. A washbasin, laundry tub, basket, or frying pan would do. Then collect the yellow specks that settle in the bottom. But to wash a pan a miner had to squat and keep his hands in icy water. A ton of "dirt" might yield an ounce of gold. It was backbreaking work, especially hard for anyone not used to manual labor. Prospectors often waded knee-deep in water to work. Some used their pants as sacks. They lugged dirt in them by tying the legs of their trousers together.

> ## "Picks and shovels were the usual tools for uncovering buried treasure."

A *rocker*, also called *cradle*, was quicker than panning. The rocker is a wooden box, open at one end and closed at the other, mounted on rockers. Cleats called "riffles" are nailed to the open end to catch gold. Sand is shoveled in and water poured through while the cradle is rocked violently. A *Long Tom* is an enlarged rocker, eight to twenty feet long. At least three people are needed: one to shovel dirt into it, a second to pour water over the dirt, and a third to rock the big cradle. The Long Tom can handle a lot of dirt, but it needs continuous fast-moving water. This means that miners have to be near a river, or dig a ditch that will bring water to their diggings.

Working the Long Tom

Building a *dam* across a stream sounded sensible. Wall off the water; expose a gold-paved bottom. However, making a dam meant working in freezing waters while carrying heavy timbers and boulders that were needed for construction. And even these efforts didn't guarantee results.[7] Only a few dams were made in 1849; by 1850, rivers were cluttered with them.

Pans, rockers, and dams weren't needed for a few diving bell enthusiasts. They brought along their gear, put on their metal helmets, and jumped into streams and rivers holding crowbars to pry gold loose. When they sank, their expectations usually did, too.

> *"Only a few dams were made in 1849; by 1850, rivers were cluttered with them."*

Dry diggings in ravines and hillsides were usual workplaces. Groups often resorted to *coyoting:* burrowing long tunnels into hills and sinking shafts into the ground. Many people were crushed and killed by cave-ins. Eventually, "coyoters" reinforced tunnels with wood beams.

Finding a fortune was as chancy as picking a winning lottery number. A disheartened, disappointed miner sent this message home: "Say to all my friends: stay at home. Tell my enemies to come."[8]

Notes

1. Oscar Lewis, *Sutter's Fort: Gateway to the Gold Fields* (Englewood Cliffs, N.J.: Prentice-Hall, 1966), 165.

2. Estimates vary because no one kept accurate records at that time.

3. In 1849, the year after San Francisco's two newspapers had been shut down because their staffs had left for the mines, the *Alta California* newspaper was published in San Francisco. Subsequently many mining towns had their own newspapers.

4. Bayard Taylor, *Eldorado or Adventures in the Path of Empire* (New York: Alfred A. Knopf, 1949), 85. This story about laundry being shipped to China and Hawaii seems hard to believe. Although it was reported by Taylor, some historians suspect that he may have neglected to verify it.

5. Elisha Douglas Perkins, *Gold Rush Diary: Being the Journal of Elisha Douglas Perkins on the Overland Trail in the Spring and Summer of 1849* (Lexington, KY.: University of Kentucky Press, 1967), 165 (Letter of Samuel Cross, Oct. 6, 1849).

6. The northern mines referred to the Feather, Yuba, Bear, and American rivers. The southern mines were located along the Cosumnes, Mokelumne, Calaveras, Stanislaus, Tuolumne, and Mariposa rivers.

7. Alonzo Delano, a prospector from Illinois, helped build two dams. One was never finished. The other cost sixteen thousand dollars to build and produced no gold. Delano wrote that several groups invested eight thousand dollars each building dams, and not one paid off.

8. J. S. Holliday, *The World Rushed In: The California Gold Rush Experience* (New York: Simon and Schuster, 1981), 350.

Looking for Clues

by Rhoda Blumberg

Adventure stories are always entertaining, and for me true stories from history are the most exciting of all.

I have always been intrigued by the great California Gold Rush because it is about ordinary people like us who set out to seek their fortunes. Some looked for gold, expecting to "get rich quick." Others headed West on dreams of finding happier, better lives.

After gold was discovered in California in 1848, the metal acted like a magic magnet. It caused people to leave their families, jobs, shops, or farms to head West. They couldn't resist newspaper reports about rocks of solid gold and glittering nuggets that were free for the taking.

I spent over a year reading their stories from primary sources: letters, diaries, old newspapers, and books. There are hundreds of fascinating accounts about the Gold Rush. Keeping diaries gave travelers and miners pleasure in self-expression and helped them forget the bad times.

I was shocked by guidebooks that had been published for travelers journeying to California. Many best-sellers were hastily written by authors who had never left home. *The Gold Regions of California, Three Weeks in the Gold Mines,* and *California: Her Wealth and Resources* were filled with promise—and not a note of good sense.

Routes recommended in some books were useless, misleading, and dangerous. Imagine being guided by mythical maps of North America that did not show the mountains or the deserts. One false chart of the day showed paved roads from Texas to the West Coast.

> *"... for me true stories from history are the most exciting of all."*

Newspaper advertisements from 1849 through the 1850s were another good source of information. In addition to pickaxes, shovels, and gold washers, California-bound adventurers were urged to buy rifles and pistols for protection against so-called "wild Indians." With few exceptions, however, Indians aided lost travelers, and supplied them with food—even though they probably resented strangers camping on their lands.

I also depended upon secondary sources: encyclopedias, books about the Gold Rush, and books about conditions during the 19th century. For example, by looking up "Death Valley" in the *Brittanica Junior*, I learned that it was named after gold seekers who lost their way and starved to death in this desert basin. After reading *Blacks in Gold Rush California* by Rudolph Lapp, I included the story of a slave who accompanied his master to the mines. He dug up enough gold to buy freedom for himself, his wife, and his two daughters. *The Far Western Frontier* by Ray Billington taught me that in 1849 Indians had no political or legal rights. They were foreigners on United States property who could not vote, own land, or expect protection from attacks.

After going through many history books, I found out about the hardships of California-bound women. They not only cooked and took care of children, but also collected buffalo dung for fuel, built campfires, yoked oxen, helped push broken-down wagons, and indulged in other "unladylike labors" not considered suitable for "delicate, sheltered females." Quite a few looked upon California as their land of opportunity, where they could dig for gold on their own, start their own businesses, and enjoy freedom from the restraints society imposed upon them.

Through research I track down information like a detective who looks for clues. Then I indulge in the happy occupation of writing about thrilling and inspiring events that really took place.

Rhoda Blumberg

Thinking About It

1 You have an opportunity to go West to make your fortune in 1850. Will you look for gold, be a shopkeeper, or what?

2 In the 1850s, "California was not only a land of riches, but also a place of freedom." Based on what you've read, would you say this is a true statement? Why or why not?

3 Read the song on pages D•84 and D•85. Suppose you are going to use this version of "Oh, Susanna" as music for a scene in a play or movie about the Gold Rush. What might happen in the scene? How would the song be performed?

More from Rhoda Blumberg

Rhoda Blumberg wrote *First Ladies of the United States.* It's the scoop on all of them, starting with Martha; you know, Martha *Washington.* Now you can find out everything you ever wanted to know about the First Ladies of our land.

Oh, Susanna

These humorous words are not the original lyrics to this song. They were written for a young man as he sailed off to find gold in California on the ship *Eliza*. This is considered the theme song of the Gold Rush.

Words Traditional U.S.A.
California Gold Rush Version
Music by Stephen Foster, 1848

I came from Salem City
With my washpan on my knee,
I'm going to California,
The gold dust for to see.
It rained all night the day I left,
The weather it was dry,
The sun so hot I froze to death,
Oh brothers, don't you cry!

(Chorus)

Oh, Susanna,
Don't you cry for me!
I'm going to California,
With my washpan on my knee!

I jumped aboard the *'Liza* ship
And traveled on the sea,
And every time I thought of home,
I wished it wasn't me!
The vessel reared like any horse,
That had of oats a wealth,
I found it wouldn't throw me so
I thought I'd throw myself!

(Chorus)

I thought of all the pleasant times
We've had together here,
I thought I ought to cry a bit,
But couldn't find a tear.
The pilot's bread* was in my mouth,
The gold dust in my eye,
And though I'm going far away,
Dear brothers, don't you cry!
*(hard tack)

(Chorus)

I soon shall be in Frisco
And there I'll look around,
And when I see the gold lumps there,
I'll pick them off the ground.
I'll scrape the mountains clean, my boys,
I'll drain the rivers dry,
A pocketful of rocks bring home,
So brothers, don't you cry!

(Chorus)

CLARA

Born: 1803

Died: 1885

S hoo!" said the old woman. "Get out of here!" A neighbor's pig had gotten into her garden again. Aunt Clara Brown shook her broom, and the fat, dirty pig waddled away. The animal trotted past a few tiny wooden houses and disappeared. In another yard, chickens were pecking and clucking about, the sound of barking dogs could be heard.

Aunt Clara sighed. They called this place Central City, but it was not much of a city at all. A few rows of small houses clung to the side of a steep hill. Down below, on Main Street, were the town's few businesses. Most of them were saloons.

BROWN

from BLACK HEROES
OF THE WILD WEST *by Ruth Pelz*

Clara looked down the dirt street. After a rain, that street was nothing but mud. Aunt Clara and the other women lifted up their long skirts and walked with care.

Of course, there weren't many women in Central City then. The rough Colorado mining towns were mostly full of men. These men spent their days in the mountains, looking for gold and silver or working in the mines. They came to town to eat and drink and gamble. Often fights started. Mining towns were some of the wildest places in the Wild West.

Aunt Clara was more than 60 years old, but she worked harder than a woman half her age. She kept busy doing the work that men didn't want to do. She opened a laundry. She washed the miners' clothes. She worked as a nurse. She started the first Sunday school. Pretty soon everyone in town knew her as someone who would lend a helping hand.

EVERYONE IN TOWN KNEW HER AS SOMEONE WHO WOULD LEND A HELPING HAND.

Clara Brown knew how important help could be. There had been many times when she could have used some help herself. As she went back to her washing, she thought about the experiences that had brought her here.

Memories of the early days were painful. She had been born a slave, in Virginia, in 1803. Slaves didn't have anything, she thought sadly. They didn't even have their families. One by one, Clara's husband and children had been taken from her and sold. Clara herself was sold many times before she was able to buy her freedom. Someday she was going to find her family and buy their freedom too. That was the dream that brought her to Central City.

SHE HAD BEEN BORN A SLAVE, IN VIRGINIA, IN 1803.

How she remembered those early stories of the gold in California and later in Colorado! For blacks and whites alike, the West seemed a land of promise. Aunt Clara Brown began to think of going west herself. Finally she had her chance. She found a group of miners who would hire her as a cook. At the age of 59, she left Missouri in a wagon train.

Two months later, she arrived in Denver. There she helped start a Sunday school. But she knew that the greatest opportunities lay in the mining towns. Central City was one of the busiest, and Clara Brown decided to settle there.

Aunt Clara had done well. She made quite a bit of money. She managed to save $10,000 from the earnings of her laundry business along with investments she had made in mining shares. As she hung up the clothes to dry, Clara dreamed again of what she would do with all that money.

She would find her family. She would buy a covered wagon and bring them all to Central City. She would build a fine house with a big yard.

Her dreams were interrupted by a noise in the street. "Oh dear," thought Clara. "Not that pig again!" She went out to look.

It was a neighbor running excitedly down the street. "Mrs. Brown!" he cried. "The War Between the States is over. The Union has won!" The man continued down the street, sharing his news with everyone he met.

Clara Brown felt a shiver of excitement. Her hands were trembling. "Now!" she said to herself. "Now I can begin."

Over the next few years, she searched for her family in every way she could. She found 34 distant relatives. She helped them and many other African Americans to come west in wagon trains. But she never found her husband or her children.

SHE SEARCHED FOR HER FAMILY IN EVERY WAY THAT SHE COULD.

The people of Central City became her family. She never refused help to a person in need, black or white. Wealthy and well-respected, Clara Brown was known as one of the town's leading citizens. At the very end of her life, this determined woman received one last wonderful surprise. One of her daughters finally found her. A part of her dream had at last come true.

THINKING
ABOUT IT

1

You are Clara Brown. Your long-lost daughter
has just found you. What are you going to tell
her first?

2

The author often calls Clara Brown "Aunt
Clara." Why do you think she does that?

3

Clara Brown made the most of opportunities
and never gave up hope. Let's name
something "The Clara Brown." What could it
be and why?

The Search for the Magic Lake

A Folk Tale from Ecuador

By Genevieve Barlow

ong ago there was a ruler of the vast Inca Empire who had an only son. This youth brought great joy to his father's heart but also a sadness, for the prince had been born in ill health.

As the years passed the prince's health did not improve, and none of the court doctors could find a cure for his illness.

One night the aged emperor went down on his knees and prayed at the altar.

"O Great Ones," he said, "I am getting older and will soon leave my people and join you in the heavens. There is no one to look after them but my son, the prince. I pray you make him well and strong so he can be a fit ruler for my people. Tell me how his malady can be cured."

The emperor put his head in his hands and waited for an answer. Soon he heard a voice coming from the fire that burned constantly in front of the altar.

"Let the prince drink water from the magic lake at the end of the world," the voice said, "and he will be well."

At that moment the fire sputtered and died. Among the cold ashes lay a golden flask.

But the emperor was much too old to make the long journey to the end of the world, and the young prince was too ill to travel. So the emperor proclaimed that whosoever should fill the golden flask with the magic water would be greatly rewarded.

Many brave men set out to search for the magic lake, but none could find it. Days and weeks passed and still the flask remained empty.

*I*n a valley, some distance from the emperor's palace, lived a poor farmer who had a wife, two grown sons, and a young daughter.

One day the older son said to his father, "Let my brother and me join in the search for the magic lake. Before the moon is new again, we shall return and help you harvest the corn and potatoes."

The father remained silent. He was not thinking of the harvest, but feared for his sons' safety.

When the father did not answer, the second son added, "Think of the rich reward, Father!"

"It is their duty to go," said his wife, "for we must all try to help our emperor and the young prince."

After his wife had spoken, the father yielded.

"Go if you must, but beware of the wild beasts and evil spirits," he cautioned.

With their parents' blessing, and an affectionate farewell from their young sister, the sons set out on their journey.

They found many lakes, but none where the sky touched the water.

Finally the younger brother said, "Before another day has passed we must return to help father with the harvest."

"Yes," agreed the other, "but I have thought of a plan. Let us each carry a jar of water from any lake along the way. We can say it will cure the prince. Even if it doesn't, surely the emperor will give us a small reward for our trouble."

"Agreed," said the younger brother.

On arriving at the palace, the deceitful youths told the emperor and his court that they brought water from the magic lake. At once the prince was given a sip from each of the brothers' jars, but of course he remained as ill as before.

"Perhaps the water must be sipped from the golden flask," one of the high priests said.

But the golden flask would not hold the water. In some mysterious way the water from the jars disappeared as soon as it was poured into the flask.

In despair the emperor called for his magician and said to him, "Can you break the spell of the flask so the water will remain for my son to drink?"

"I cannot do that, your majesty," replied the magician. "But I believe," he added wisely, "that the flask is telling us that we have been deceived by the two brothers. The flask can be filled only with water from the magic lake."

When the brothers heard this, they trembled with fright, for they knew their falsehood was discovered.

So angry was the emperor that he ordered the brothers thrown into chains. Each day they were forced to drink water from their jars as a reminder of their false deed. News of their disgrace spread far and wide.

Again the emperor sent messengers throughout the land pleading for someone to bring the magic water before death claimed him and the young prince.

Súmac, the little sister of the deceitful youths, was tending her flock of llamas when she heard the sound of the royal trumpet. Then came the voice of the emperor's servant with his urgent message from the court.

Quickly the child led her llamas home and begged her parents to let her go in search of the magic water.

"You are too young," her father said. "Besides, look at what has already befallen your brothers. Some evil spirit must have taken hold of them to make them tell such a lie."

And her mother said, "We could not bear to be without our precious Súmac!"

"But think how sad our emperor will be if the young prince dies," replied the innocent child. "And if I can find the magic lake, perhaps the emperor will forgive my brothers and send them home."

"Dear husband," said Súmac's mother, "maybe it is the will of the gods that we let her go."

Once again the father gave his permission.

"It is true," he murmured, "I must think of our emperor."

Súmac was overjoyed, and went skipping out to the corral to harness one of her pet llamas. It would carry her provisions and keep her company.

Meanwhile her mother filled a little woven bag with food and drink for Súmac—toasted golden kernels of corn and a little earthen jar of *chicha*, a beverage made from crushed corn.

The three embraced each other tearfully before Súmac set out bravely on her mission, leading her pet llama along the trail.

The first night she slept, snug and warm against her llama, in the shelter of a few rocks. But when she heard the hungry cry of the puma, she feared for her pet animal and bade it return safely home.

The next night she spent in the top branches of a tall tree, far out of reach of the dreadful puma. She hid

her provisions in a hole in the tree trunk.

At sunrise she was aroused by the voices of gentle sparrows resting on a nearby limb.

"Poor child," said the oldest sparrow, "she can never find her way to the lake."

"Let us help her," chorused the others.

"Oh please do!" implored the child, "and forgive me for intruding in your tree."

"We welcome you," chirped another sparrow, "for you are the same little girl who yesterday shared your golden corn with us."

"We shall help you," continued the first sparrow, who was the leader, "for you are a good child. Each of us will give you a wing feather, and you must hold them all together in one hand as a fan. The feathers have magic powers that will carry you wherever you wish to go. They will also protect you from harm."

Each sparrow then lifted a wing, sought out a special feather hidden underneath, and gave it to Súmac. She fashioned them into the shape of a little fan, taking the ribbon from her hair to bind the feathers together so none would be lost.

"I must warn you," said the oldest sparrow, "that the lake is guarded by three terrible creatures. But have no fear. Hold the magic fan up to your face and you will be unharmed."

Súmac thanked the birds over and over again. Then, holding up the fan in her chubby hands, she said politely, "Please, magic fan, take me to the lake at the end of the world."

A soft breeze swept her out of the top branches of the tree and through the valley. Then up she was carried, higher and higher into the sky, until she could look down and see the great mountain peaks covered with snow.

At last the wind put her down on the shore of a beautiful lake. It was, indeed, the lake at the end of the world, for, on the opposite side from where she stood, the sky came down so low it touched the water.

Súmac tucked the magic fan into her waistband and ran to the edge of the water. Suddenly her face fell. She had left everything back in the forest. What could she use for carrying the precious water back to the prince?

"Oh, I do wish I had remembered the jar!" she said, weeping.

Suddenly she heard a soft thud in the sand at her feet. She looked down and discovered a beautiful golden flask—the same one the emperor had found in the ashes.

Súmac took the flask and kneeled at the water's edge. Just then a hissing voice behind her said, "Get away from my lake or I shall wrap my long, hairy legs around your neck."

Súmac turned around. There stood a giant crab as large as a pig and as black as night.

With trembling hands the child took the magic fan from her waistband and spread it open in front of her face. As soon as the crab looked at it, he closed his eyes and fell down on the sand in a deep sleep.

Once more Súmac started to fill the flask. This time she was startled by a fierce voice bubbling up from the water.

"Get away from my lake or I shall eat you," gurgled a giant green alligator. His long tail beat the water angrily.

Súmac waited until the creature swam closer. Then she held up the fan. The alligator blinked. He drew back. Slowly, quietly, he sank to the bottom of the lake in a sound sleep.

AGAIN SUMAC'S FAN SAVED HER FROM HARM.

Before Súmac could recover from her fright, she heard a shrill whistle in the air. She looked up and saw a flying serpent. His skin was red as blood. Sparks flew from his eyes.

"Get away from my lake or I shall bite you," hissed the serpent as it batted its wings around her head.

Again Súmac's fan saved her from harm. The serpent closed his eyes and drifted to the ground. He folded his wings and coiled up on the sand. Then he began to snore.

Súmac sat for a moment to quiet herself. Then, realizing that the danger was past, she sighed with great relief.

"Now I can fill the golden flask and be on my way," she said to herself.

When this was done, she held the flask tightly in one hand and clutched the fan in the other.

"Please take me to the palace," she said.

Hardly were the words spoken, when she found herself safely in front of the palace gates. She looked at the tall guard.

"I wish to see the emperor," Súmac uttered in trembling tones.

"Why, little girl?" the guard asked kindly.

"I bring water from the magic lake to cure the prince."

The guard looked down at her in astonishment.

"Come!" he commanded in a voice loud and deep as thunder.

In just a few moments Súmac was led into a room full of sadness. The emperor was pacing up and down in despair. The prince lay motionless on a huge bed. His eyes were closed and his face was without color. Beside him knelt his mother, weeping.

Without wasting words, Súmac went to the prince and gave him a few drops of magic water. Soon he opened his eyes. His cheeks became flushed. It was not long before he sat up in bed. He drank some more.

"How strong I feel!" the prince cried joyfully.

The emperor and his wife embraced Súmac. Then Súmac told them of her adventurous trip to the lake. They praised her courage. They marveled at the reappearance of the golden flask and at the powers of the magic fan.

"Dear child," said the emperor, "all the riches of my empire are not enough to repay you for saving my son's life. Ask what you will and it shall be yours."

"Oh, generous emperor," said Súmac timidly, "I have but three wishes."

"Name them and they shall be yours," urged the emperor.

"First, I wish my brothers to be free to return to my parents. They have learned their lesson and will never be false again. I know they were only thinking of a reward for my parents. Please forgive them."

"Guards, free them at once!" ordered the emperor.

"Secondly, I wish the magic fan returned to the forest so the sparrows may have their feathers again."

This time the emperor had no time to speak. Before anyone in the room could utter a sound, the magic fan lifted itself up, spread itself wide open, and floated out the window toward the woods. Everyone watched in amazement. When the fan was out of sight, they applauded.

"What is your last wish, dear Súmac?" asked the queen mother.

"I wish that my parents be given a large farm and great flocks of llamas, vicuñas, and alpacas, so they will not be poor any longer."

"It will be so," said the emperor, "but I am sure your parents never considered themselves poor with so wonderful a daughter."

"Won't you stay with us in the palace?" ventured the prince.

"Yes, stay with us!" urged the emperor and his wife. "We will do everything to make you happy."

"Oh thank you," said Súmac blushing happily, "but I must return to my parents and to my brothers. I miss them as I know they have missed me. They do not even know I am safe, for I came directly to your palace."

The royal family did not try to detain Súmac any longer.

"My own guard will see that you get home safely," said the emperor.

When she reached home, she found that all she had wished for had come to pass: her brothers were waiting for her with their parents; a beautiful house and huge barn were being constructed; her father had received a deed granting him many acres of new, rich farmland.

Súmac ran into the arms of her happy family.

At the palace, the golden flask was never empty. Each time it was used, it was refilled. Thus the prince's royal descendants never suffered ill health and the kingdom remained strong.

But it is said that when the Spanish conqueror of the ancient Incas demanded a room filled with golden gifts, the precious flask was among them. Whatever happened to this golden treasure is unknown, for the conqueror was killed and the Indians wandered over the mainland in search of a new leader. Some say the precious gifts—including the golden flask—are buried at the bottom of the lake at the end of the world, but no one besides Súmac has ever ventured to go there.

THINKING ABOUT IT

1 Three wishes, three wishes, three wishes. Have you heard about three wishes before reading this story? Why are there so often three wishes in a story? Are there ever three wishes in real life? What do you think about this matter?

2 Súmac offers two reasons why she must go to the Magic Lake. Which reason is more important to Súmac? Which reason convinces her parents to let her go? Justify your response.

3 You're about to journey to an unknown destination in search of . . . ??? What will you be looking for? What will you bring with you? What else do you need to think about to get ready for this trip? Make your plans now!

Another Folk Tale
Try *Potatoes, Potatoes* by Anita Lobel. This is a tale of two brothers who won't stop fighting and a wise mother who won't stop trying to make peace.

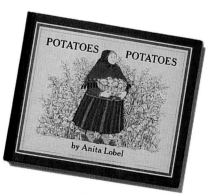

THE MAGIC

魔法のふるい

SIEVE

CAST

NARRATOR Male / Female

SISTER Female

BROTHER Male

HIS WIFE Female

FISHERWOMAN Female

GOBLIN 1 Male / Female

GOBLIN 2 Male / Female

GOBLIN 3 Male / Female

GOBLIN 4 Male / Female

GOBLIN 5 Male / Female

NEIGHBORS 1 to 5 Male / Female
   (may be double-cast as the goblins)

SPIRIT OF THE SIEVE Male / Female

STAGING

The boat may be represented by an upturned bench or a riser, and may remain on stage throughout.

A pair of bamboo screens set upstage are useful for entrances and exits, and are sufficient to suggest various locations.

PROPS

Charcoal brazier (a low waste-paper basket), one for each family.
Jewelry.
A large sieve.
A log of wood.
A corncake or muffin.
A fishing net or rope.
A tatami or woven mat.
A small bowl.
A white sheet or cloth.
A fan (optional).

In Kabuki theatre, the folding fan is considered a very important prop because of its flexibility: held open, half-shut, or closed, it represents a variety of moods and objects. When closed, it can become a knife, a pen, or any long, thin object.

The goblins may be played by actors holding small stick masks. In one recent production, the students cut out face shapes from felt pieces, gave each a "goblin-like appearance," then stiffened the faces by backing them on to pieces of cardboard, and stapling the whole to the front of twelve-inch pieces of dowel.

COSTUMES

Simple clothes. If available, short kimonos.

The Spirit of the Sieve should wear something white.

The Fisherwoman (who, in some productions, may be double-cast as the Spirit of the Sieve) needs a large, shabby shawl.

THE MAGIC SIEVE

BASED ON A JAPANESE FOLKTALE
by Irene N. Watts

When the play opens, the two families are already on stage, side by side, separated by an imaginary thin wall between their houses. The characters are frozen, until each one begins to speak. The wealth of the sister may be suggested by her dress and jewels.

NARRATOR: Two relatives, whose fortunes had separated, prepared to welcome in the New Year.

BROTHER: The brother . . .

WIFE: His wife . . .

SISTER: And his sister . . .

NARRATOR: Lived next door to each other.

SISTER: The sister was very rich and had many things.

Sister puts on necklace and rings.

BROTHER: But her brother was poor; he did not even have enough coal left in his hibachi to heat his home.

The sister warms herself at her fire. The couple shivers.

WIFE: His wife longed to make rice cakes to celebrate the New Year, but alas, she had no rice. She asked her husband, "Please take this empty bowl and ask your sister, as a special favor, to lend us some rice."

Freeze.

BROTHER: So the brother went next door *(he bows)*. "We have no rice for New Year's breakfast. Will you lend us just a little? I will return it as soon as I can."

SISTER: I have none to spare *(turns him away)*.

He exits from the sister's house. Depending on staging, sister and wife should exit during next speech, removing any props with them.

BROTHER: The brother was ashamed to return home to his wife empty-handed. He decided to walk for a while. He took the path towards the sea. The day was as cold as his sister's words.

FISHERWOMAN: A fisherwoman was mending her nets. Her fingers were old and clumsy. She said, "Please, young man, help me turn my net."

BROTHER: Gladly.

FISHERWOMAN: Thank you, the net is heavy for my
fingers. You are kind. Tell me, why do you look so
sad? Don't you know that tomorrow is the New
Year?

BROTHER: Yes, but my wife and I go hungry, while others
celebrate. The world is a cold and selfish place.

FISHERWOMAN: Not all the world is bad. You helped me;
now I will help you in return. Take this corncake and
go back along the path until you reach the
mountains. Wait quietly, and you will see the
mountain men. They will beg you for that cake. You
may give it to them *only* in exchange for their sieve.
Don't forget.

She exits.

BROTHER: The young man bowed his thanks and began to
walk towards the mountains.

Goblins appear.

NARRATOR: A noise like a swarm of bees around a hive
filled the air.

BROTHER: Those must be the mountain men the
fisherwoman told me about. How noisy they are! I
did not know they were goblins. They seem to be
quarreling. I'll wait here and watch.

*Goblins shout and push each other, trying to lift a log from a
hole in the ground. They turn and see the brother and begin
to drag him to the hole.*

GOBLIN 1: A goblin was trapped there, and cried, "Help, murder, I'm caught under this log!"

BROTHER: The young man quickly freed him. "There you are," he said.

GOBLIN 1: The goblin did not bother to thank him. "I must have that corncake in your pocket; it smells better than all the things I have ever eaten."

BROTHER: The young man remembered what he had been told and said, "No, I cannot part with it."

NARRATOR: All the other goblins came 'round and offered him bribes for the cake.

GOBLIN 2: Give us the cake for our dinner and you shall have a bag of gold.

GOBLINS: Gold, gold, gold.

BROTHER: But the man would not change his mind. "I'll not exchange this cake for all the gold on the mountain."

NARRATOR: The goblins whispered together, greedily.

GOBLIN 3: "Not for all our mountain gold?" asked one.

GOBLIN 4: "That must be a very special cake," said another.

GOBLIN 5: "What *will* you take for it?" pleaded the last.

BROTHER: The man looked around, pretending to consider for a long time, then he spoke: "I'll give you this special corncake for . . . "

GOBLINS: Yes, yes, go on, for what?

BROTHER: In exchange for the sieve in which you shake the mountain earth.

NARRATOR: The goblins put their heads together and argued loudly, but at last they said:

GOBLINS: We are all agreed.

The brother holds out the cake temptingly, just out of the goblins' reach. One of them holds out the sieve.

GOBLIN 1: Here is our magic sieve. It cannot give you gold, but it will give you anything else that you really need. Treat it well.

GOBLIN 2: When you make a wish, you must turn the sieve to the right . . .

GOBLIN 5: And when you have enough, then . . .

GOBLIN 3: Turn the sieve to the left.

GOBLIN 4: And don't forget to say, "Stop, sieve, stop."

GOBLIN 1: Here.

Grabs the cake and runs, with other goblins.

NARRATOR: And all the goblins ran with it into the mountains, and were never seen again.

BROTHER: Holding the precious sieve, the brother went home.

WIFE: His wife had been waiting anxiously for his return, for it was getting dark and cold. "Where have you been for so long? It is almost New Year. I hope you have brought the rice."

BROTHER: I have brought you something much better than a bowl of rice. Here is a magic sieve that will give us whatever we really need. Let's try it right away.

NARRATOR: They spread a clean tatami mat and put the sieve on it.

WIFE: Sieve, sieve, please make us some rice.

BROTHER: And he turned it to the right.

WIFE: The wife was amazed to see so much rice appear, enough for many meals.

BROTHER: Then her husband turned the sieve to the left, and said, "Stop, sieve, stop."

WIFE: This is a wonderful magic sieve. Let's share our good fortune and make a New Year's feast for all our friends and neighbors. And of course, we'll invite your sister too.

NARRATOR: All their neighbors and friends came and enjoyed the feast.

大晚餐

NEIGHBOR 1: What excellent food, such tasty fish and chicken!

NEIGHBOR 2: How kind of you to share your good fortune!

NEIGHBOR 3: You must have worked hard to provide all this for us.

NEIGHBOR 4: A feast to remember.

NEIGHBOR 5: May fortune be with you all through the years.

WIFE: Indeed.

BROTHER: The brother said, "It is nothing at all. There is plenty more for all of you, as much as you can eat."

SISTER: The sister looked on and was so full of envy that she could not eat. How could her brother afford all this, and where did it come from?

She asked her brother, "Did you have a big catch yesterday after all?"

BROTHER: An old fisherwoman showed me a lucky place. Thank you for honoring us with your presence.

The neighbors bow and leave, followed by the sister, looking doubtful.

SISTER: This time she had to turn away, but she determined to discover her brother's secret. That night, when all was quiet, she waited outside in the darkness and looked and listened.

She holds an open fan—the "wall" at which she listens.

WIFE: The wife put the sieve in a safe place and said, "Thank you for your magic gifts." And then she went to sleep.

The couple exits or sleeps.

SISTER: The sister crept into the house and stole the sieve. She walked down to the sea and climbed into a boat that she kept there. She rowed out to sea so that she could not be seen or heard.

"I'll wish for gold," she said, and started to shake the sieve as hard as she could. "Make gold for me, lots of gold . . . "

The spirit of the sieve appears upstage.

SPIRIT OF THE SIEVE: Those who wish gold from me will get white salt to fill the sea.

NARRATOR: Then the sieve started to make salt.

SISTER: Who spoke? I have been tricked. I want gold, not salt! Help me, the salt is too heavy for the boat. It will sink! Stop, help me!

SIEVE: But the sieve went on pouring salt, and soon the boat was covered in white salt. Slowly the boat and the selfish sister and the magic sieve sank to the bottom of the sea.

The spirit and the sister sink in slow motion to the ground, covered by a white cloth that the spirit places over them. Freeze.

NARRATOR: The sieve is still making salt, and that is why the sea will always taste salty.

Pulling the Theme Together

1

Take part in *The Magic Sieve*. What role will you play? Will you go along with the basic story or will you attempt to change it?

2

Folk tales are usually simple, with lots of action. They often contain advice about how to live wisely. Are there any modern-day folk tales? Where would you find one? If you made up a folk tale of today, what would it be about?

3

People write stories, poems, and articles about what is important to them. Whom or what would you write about if you were contributing to *Within My Reach*?

Books to Enjoy

Gold
by Milton Meltzer
HarperCollins, 1993
This is the true story of why people search, mine, trade, steal, mint, hoard, shape, wear, and fight and kill for gold.

Zeely
by Virginia Hamilton
Macmillan, 1967
Elizabeth creates a new identity for herself and tells stories about Zeely, the African queen.

. . . and now Miguel
by Joseph Krumgold
Crowell, 1953
Miguel's story is based on a real one, about a boy growing up on a sheep ranch. Sheepherding is fun, but is it more responsibility than a boy can handle?

Trouble at the Mines
by Doreen Rappaport
Crowell, 1987
Picture this: over one hundred years ago, a grandmother led a coal miner's strike.

Dawn

by Molly Bang
William Morrow, 1983
Trust me; I'll weave beautiful sails for you. But don't look in on me while I'm weaving. If you do, we'll both be sorry at dawn.

The Real Thief

by William Steig
Farrar, Straus & Giroux, 1973
It really hurts when Gawain gets blamed for something he didn't do . . . and winds up losing his job because of it.

All the Money in the World

by Bill Brittain
Harper, 1979
All the money in the world is in Quentin's backyard: what on earth is he going to do with it?

Exploring the Titanic

by Robert D. Ballard
Madison Press, 1988
Step by step, dive by dive, the author tells you exactly how he found the long-lost Titanic on the North Atlantic floor. His photographs give you an eerie feeling of being there.

Literary Terms

Expository Nonfiction

Expository nonfiction provides you with facts. The author has done a great deal of research to find those facts. The materials the author uses are called primary sources. "Land of Promise" is expository nonfiction because it is the factual history of the California Gold Rush. In "Looking for Clues," Rhoda Blumberg mentions several book and manuscript collections in which she located illustrations for her book. She also tells how she used other primary sources, such as letters, for information about the Gold Rush.

Folk Tale

A **folk tale** is a story that was told long ago by storytellers. Almost all folk tales involve some magic and a struggle between good and evil. In the case of "The Search for the Magic Lake" and *The Magic Sieve*, good conquers evil and the stories end happily. This is the usual form for a folk tale.

Foreshadowing

Foreshadowing is an author's way of giving you clues about what might happen later in a story.

Often it creates suspense about what is going to happen. In "Skybird to the High Heavens," Rosa tells her grandmother about her dream of riding on the back of a quetzel. Her grandmother warns Rosa that the dream may be telling her she will have to hide from danger. When soldiers burn the village, Rosa does run until she finds safety in a refugee camp. The dream and her grandmother's interpretation of it are a foreshadowing of what will happen.

Mood

Mood is the feeling of a story. It can reflect the actions that take place. The mood in "A Fair Trade" is one of suspense. Will the dog go home or continue to follow the wagon? Will his owner, Jeb Grimes, take him back? Will the sheriff arrest Pa for stealing the dog? All the questions in your mind as you read the story set the mood of suspense.

Parody

A **parody** is a new version of an old song or story. "Oh, Susanna" is the gold-miner's version of the old familiar song that begins, "I came from Alabama with my banjo on my knee." A parody is usually amusing, as in the first line of the gold-miner's version: "I came from Salem City with my wash-pan on my knee."

Sarcasm

Sarcasm is a type of humor in which a person makes fun of what someone else has said or done. In "The Night Sky over Kansas," Jacob tells the newsstand attendant that he lost his keys. "So you want a newspaper that tells you where to find them?" is the sarcastic response. When Jacob's mother asks how he's feeling, Jacob replies that he's a little tired because he had to turn the volume knob (on the TV) way up, and it took a lot out of him. This kind of sarcasm is meant to put the other person down.

Glossary

Vocabulary from your selections

ar go naut (är′gə nôt), **1** (in Greek legends) any of the men who sailed with Jason in search of the Golden Fleece. **2** person who went to California in 1849 in search of gold. *n.*

asth ma (az′mə), a chronic disease characterized by difficulty in breathing accompanied by wheezing, a feeling of suffocation, and coughing. *n.*

bribe (brīb), **1** money or other reward given or offered to a person to do something dishonest, unlawful, etc.: *The driver who caused the accident offered the police officer a bribe to let her go.* **2** a reward for doing something that a person does not want to do: *The stubborn child needed a bribe to go to bed.* **3** give or offer a bribe to: *A gambler bribed one of the boxers to lose the fight.* **1,2** *n.,* **3** *v.,* **bribed, brib ing.** —**brib′a ble,** *adj.* —**brib′er,** *n.*

brilliant

bril liant (bril′yənt), **1** shining brightly; sparkling: *brilliant jewels, brilliant sunshine.* **2** splendid; magnificent: *The singer gave a brilliant performance.* **3** having great ability: *a brilliant musician.* **4** diamond or other gem cut to sparkle brightly. **1-3** *adj.,* **4** *n.* —**bril′liant ly,** *adv.*

chron ic (kron′ik), **1** lasting a long time: *a chronic disease.* **2** never stopping; constant; habitual: *a chronic tease.* *adj.* —**chron′i cal ly,** *adv.*

de ceit ful (di sēt′fəl), **1** ready or willing to deceive or lie: *a deceitful person.* **2** meant to deceive; deceiving; misleading: *She told a deceitful story to avoid punishment. adj.* —**de ceit′ ful ly,** *adv.* —**de ceit′ful ness,** *n.*

de ceive (di sēv′), **1** make (a person) believe as true something that is false; mislead: *The magician deceived her audience into thinking she had really pulled a rabbit from a hat.* **2** use deceit; lie. *v.,* **de ceived, de ceiv ing.** —**de ceiv′a ble,** *adj.* —**de ceiv′a ble ness,** *n.* —**de ceiv′a bly,** *adv.* —**de ceiv′ing ly,** *adv.*

dis a ble (dis ā′bəl), make unable; make unfit for use, action, etc.; cripple: *A sprained wrist disabled the tennis player for three weeks. He was disabled by polio. v.,* **dis a bled, dis a bling.** —**dis a′ble ment,** *n.* —**dis a′bler,** *n.*

earn ings (ėr′ningz), money earned; wages or profits. *n., pl.*

en vy (en′vē), **1** feeling of discontent, dislike, or desire because another has what one wants: *The children were filled with envy when they saw her new bicycle.* **2** the object of such feeling; person or thing envied: *Their new car was the envy of the neighborhood.* **3** feel envy toward: *Some people envy the rich.* **4** feel envy because of: *He envied his friend's success.* **1,2** *n., pl.* **en vies; 3,4** *v.,* **en vied, en vy ing.** —**en′vy ing ly,** *adv.* [*Envy* came into English about 700 years ago from French *envie,* and can be traced back to Latin *in-,* meaning "against," and *videre,* meaning "to see."]

ex pec ta tion (ek´spek tā´shən), **1** an expecting or a being expected; anticipation: *the expectation of a good harvest.* **2** something expected. **3** good reason for expecting something; prospect: *They have expectations of money from a rich aunt. n.*

ex per i ence (ek spir´ē əns), **1** what happens to a person; what is seen, done, or lived through: *We had several pleasant experiences on our trip. People often learn by experience.* **2** knowledge or skill gained by seeing, doing, or living through things; practice: *Have you had any experience in this kind of work?* **3** have happen to one; feel: *experience great pain.* 1,2 *n.,* 3 *v.,* **ex per i enced, ex per i enc ing.**

flask (flask), a glass or metal bottle, especially one with a narrow neck. *n.*

fren zy (fren´zē), **1** a state of near madness; frantic condition: *They were in a frenzy when they heard that their child was missing.* **2** a condition of very great excitement: *The crowd was in a frenzy after the home team scored the winning goal. n., pl.* **fren zies.** [*Frenzy* came into English over 600 years ago from French *frenesie,* and can be traced back to Greek *phrēn,* meaning "the mind."]

hand bill (hand´bil´), notice or advertisement, usually printed on one page, that is to be handed out to people. *n.*

in fla tion (in flā´shən), **1** a swelling (with air or gas). **2** a swollen state; too great expansion. **3** a sharp increase in prices resulting from too great an expansion in paper money or bank credit. *n.*

in ha la tion (in´hə lā´shən), an inhaling. *n.*

in hale (in hāl´), draw (air, gas, fragrance, tobacco smoke, etc.) into the lungs; breathe in. *v.,* **in haled, in hal ing.**

a hat	i it	oi oil	ch child	ə stands for:
ā age	ī ice	ou out	ng long	a in about
ä far	o hot	u cup	sh she	e in taken
e let	ō open	u̇ put	th thin	i in pencil
ē equal	ô order	ü rule	ŦH then	o in lemon
ėr term			zh measure	u in circus

in ter rupt (in´tə rupt´), **1** break in upon (talk, work, rest, a person speaking, etc.); keep from going on; stop for a time; hinder: *A fire drill interrupted the lesson.* **2** cause a break; break in: *It is not polite to interrupt when someone is talking.* **3** make a break in: *A dam interrupts the flow of the river. v.* —**in´ter rupt´er,** *n.* —**in´ter rupt´i ble,** *adj.*

in vest ment (in vest´mənt), **1** an investing; a laying out of money: *Getting an education is a wise investment of time and money.* **2** amount of money invested: *Their investments amount to thousands of dollars.* **3** something that is expected to yield money as income or profit or both: *She has a good income from wise investments. n.*

loom (lüm), frame or machine for weaving cloth. *n.*

loom

make shift (māk′shift′), **1** something used for a time instead of the right thing; temporary substitute: *When the lights went out, we used candles as a makeshift.* **2** used for a time instead of the right thing: *makeshift awnings.* **1** *n.,* **2** *adj.*

man u al (man′yü əl), **1** of the hands; done with the hands: *manual labor.* **2** a small book that helps its readers to understand and use something; handbook. **1** *adj.,* **2** *n.* —**man′u al ly,** *adv.*

mem or y (mem′ər ē), **1** ability to remember or keep in the mind: *She will recall when that happened, for she has a good memory.* **2** act of remembering; remembrance: *My memory of the trip is still fresh.* **3** person, thing, or event that is remembered: *I was so young when we moved that our old house is only a vague memory.* **4** all that a person remembers. **5** length of past time that is remembered: *This is the hottest summer within my memory.* **6** part of a computer or computer system in which information and instructions can be stored, temporarily or permanently.* *n., pl.* **mem or ies.** [*Memory* came into English about 600 years ago from French *memorie,* and can be traced back to Latin *memor,* meaning "mindful."] **in memory of,** to help in remembering; as a reminder of: *I send you this gift in memory of our summer together.*

pat tern (pat′ərn), **1** arrangement of forms and colors; design: *the pattern of a wallpaper, a pattern of polka dots.* **2** a model or guide for something to be made: *I used a paper pattern in cutting the cloth for my coat.* **3** a fine example; model to be followed: *He was a pattern of generosity.* **4** make according to a pattern: *Pattern yourself after your mother.* **5** any arrangement: *behavior pattern, a speech pattern.* **1-3,5** *n.,* **4** *v.* —**pat′tern less,** *adj.*

pos ses sion (pə zesh′ən), **1** a possessing; holding: *I have in my possession the books you thought you'd lost.* **2** ownership: *On her 21st birthday she came into possession of 50 thousand dollars.* **3** thing possessed; property: *Please move your possessions from my room.* **4** territory under the rule of a country: *Guam is a possession of the United States.* **5** domination by a particular feeling, idea, evil spirit, etc. **6** self-control. *n.*

po ten tial (pə ten′shəl), **1** possible as opposed to actual; capable of coming into being or action: *There is a potential danger of being bitten when playing with a strange dog.* **2** something potential; possibility. **3** (in grammar) expressing possibility by the use of *may, might, can, could,* etc.: *the potential mood of a verb.* **4** amount of electrification of a point with reference to some standard. A current of high potential is used in transmitting electric power over long distances. **1,3** *adj.,* **2,4** *n.* —**po ten′tial ly,** *adv.*

prac ti cal (prak′tə kəl), **1** of action or practice rather than thought or theory: *Earning a living is a practical matter.* **2** fit for actual practice: *a practical plan.* **3** useful: *An outdoor swimming pool is more practical in Florida than in Minnesota.* **4** having good sense: *A practical person does not spend time and money foolishly.* **5** engaged in actual practice or work: *A practical farmer works a farm.* **6** being such in effect; virtual: *So many of our players were injured that our victory was a practical defeat.* *adj.* —**prac′ti cal ness,** *n.*

practical joke, trick or prank played on a person. —**practical joker.**

pre cious (presh′əs), **1** having great value; worth much; valuable. Gold, platinum, and silver are often called the precious metals. Diamonds, rubies, and sapphires are precious stones. **2** much loved; dear: *a precious child.* **3** too nice; overly refined: *precious language.* **4** very great: *a precious mess.* **5** INFORMAL. very: *precious little money.* **1-4** *adj.,* **5** *adv.* —**pre′cious ly,** *adv.* —**pre′cious ness,** *n.*

pres ence (prez′ns), **1** a being present in a place: *I just learned of her presence in the city.* **2** a place where a person is: *The messenger was admitted to the king's presence.* **3** appearance; bearing: *The queen is a person of noble presence.* **4** something present, especially a ghost, spirit, or the like. *n.*

pro vi sion (prə vizh′ən), **1** statement making a condition: *A provision of the lease is that the rent must be paid promptly.* **2** act of providing; preparation: *They made provision for their children's education.* **3** care taken for the future; arrangement made beforehand: *There is a provision for making the building larger if necessary.* **4** that which is made ready; supply; stock, especially of food; food. **5 provisions,** *pl.* a supply of food and drinks: *They took plenty of provisions on their trip.* **6** to supply with provisions: *The cabin was well provisioned with canned goods.* 1-5 *n.,* 6 *v.* —**pro vi′sion er,** *n.* —**pro vi′sion less,** *adj.*

sam ple (sam′pəl), **1** part to show what the rest is like; one thing to show what the others are like: *Here are some samples of drapery material for you to choose from.* **2** serving as an example: *a sample copy.* **3** take a part of; test a part of: *We sampled the cake and found it very good.* 1 *n.,* 2 *adj.,* 3 *v.,* **sam pled, sam pling.**

sieve (siv), **1** utensil having holes that let liquids and smaller pieces pass through, but not the larger pieces: *Shaking flour through a sieve removes lumps.* **2** put through a sieve. 1 *n.,* 2 *v.,* **sieved, siev ing.** —**sieve′like′,** *adj.*

time piece (tīm′pēs′), clock or watch. *n.*

ven ture (ven′chər), **1** a risky or daring undertaking: *Our courage was equal to any venture. A lucky venture in oil stock made him rich.* **2** expose to risk or danger: *She ventured her life to rescue me.* **3** dare: *No one ventured to interrupt the speaker.* **4** dare to come

a hat	i it	oi oil	ch child	ə stands for:
ā age	ī ice	ou out	ng long	a in about
ä far	o hot	u cup	sh she	e in taken
e let	ō open	u̇ put	th thin	i in pencil
ē equal	ô order	ü rule	ᴛʜ then	o in lemon
ėr term			zh measure	u in circus

or go: *We ventured out on the thin ice and fell through.* **5** dare to say or make: *He ventured an objection.* 1 *n.,* 2-5 *v.,* **ven tured, ven tur ing.**

weave (wēv), **1** form (threads or strips) into a thing or fabric. People weave thread into cloth, straw into hats, and reeds into baskets. **2** make out of thread, strips, or strands of the same material. A spider weaves a web. *She is weaving a rug.* **3** work with a loom. **4** method or pattern of weaving: *Homespun is a cloth of coarse weave.* 1-3 *v.,* **wove, wo ven** or **wove, weav ing;** 4 *n.*

weaving

wheeze (hwēz), **1** breathe with difficulty and a whistling sound. **2** a whistling sound caused by difficult breathing. **3** make a sound like this: *The old engine wheezed.* 1,3 *v.,* **wheezed, wheez ing;** 2 *n.* [*Wheeze* came into English over 500 years ago, probably from Icelandic *hvæsa,* meaning "to hiss."]

Acknowledgments

Text

Page 6: From *Thin Air* by David Getz, pages 1–15. Copyright © 1990 by David Getz. Reprinted by permission of Henry Holt and Company, Inc.

Page 32: From *Sports Pages* by Arnold Adoff, illustrations by Steven Kuzma. Text copyright © 1986 by Arnold Adoff. Illustrations copyright © 1986 by Steve Kuzma. Reprinted by permission of HarperCollins Publishers.

Page 36: "Skybird to the High Heavens" from *Light: Stories of a Small Kindness* by Nancy White Carlstrom. Copyright © 1990 by Nancy White Carlstrom. Reprinted by permission of Little, Brown and Company.

Page 46: From *Mr. Mysterious & Company* by Sid Fleischman, illustrations by Eric von Schmidt. Copyright © 1962, 1990 by Albert S. Fleischman. Reprinted by permission of Little, Brown and Company.

Page 61: "Story Weaving," by Sid Fleischman. Copyright © 1991 by Sid Fleischman.

Page 64: From *The Great American Gold Rush* by Rhoda Blumberg, pages 61–70, 71–87 and 116–122. Copyright © 1989 by Rhoda Blumberg. Reprinted with the permission of Simon & Schuster Books for Young Readers.

Page 80: "Looking for Clues," by Rhoda Blumberg. Copyright © 1991 by Rhoda Blumberg.

Page 84: "Oh, Susanna" from *The Laura Ingalls Wilder Songbook*, edited by Eugenia Garson. Reprinted by permission of HarperCollins Publishers.

Page 86: "Clara Brown" from *Black Heroes of the Wild West* by Ruth Pelz, illustrations by Leandro Della Piana. Copyright © 1990 by Open Hand Publishing, Inc. Reprinted by permission.

Page 92: "The Search for the Magic Lake" from *Latin American Tales* by Genevieve Barlow, 1966. Reprinted by permission of the author.

Page 110: "The Magic Sieve" from *Just a Minute: Ten Short Plays & Activities for Your Classroom* by Irene Watts. Copyright © 1989 by Irene N. Watts. Reprinted by permission of Pembroke Publishers, Ltd., Canada.

Artists

Illustrations owned and copyrighted by the illustrator.

Elizabeth Wolf, cover, 1–3
Thirst (lettering), 4, 64, 79, 80, 83
Ray Lago, 6–30
Steve Kuzma, 33, 35
José Ortega, 36–45
Eric von Schmidt, 47, 51, 57, 58
Laurie Rosenwald (lettering), 46–63
John Sandford, 84–85
Larry McEntire, 86–91
Judy Filippo, 92–109
Jewel Homad, 96, 101, 106
Satoru Igarashi, 110–127

Photographs

Page 61: Photo of Sid Fleischman courtesy of Marilyn Sanders
Pages 64, 65, 77: Courtesy California State Library, Sacramento
Pages 70–71: Courtesy Wells Fargo Bank
Page 75: Courtesy The New York Historical Society, New York City
Page 80: Courtesy of Rhoda Blumberg
Page 132: Courtesy Steve White/Photo Design
Page 133: Courtesy Museum of American Textile History
Page 135: Courtesy Walter S. Clark, Jr.

Glossary

The contents of the Glossary entries in this book have been adapted from *Intermediate Dictionary*, Copyright © 1988 Scott, Foresman and Company; and *Advanced Dictionary*, Copyright © 1988 Scott, Foresman and Company.